GOD WORKS THROUGH YOU

DR. ROBERT A. RUSSELL

Audio Enlightenment Press

Giving Voice to the Wisdom of the Ages

Printed in the United States of America

ISBN 978-1-941489-33-8

www.AudioEnlightenmentPress.com

www.MetaPhysicalPocketBooks.Com

Audio book available on iTunes

God Works Through You

Dr. Robert A. Russell

TABLE OF CONTENTS

Foreword   i

Acknowledgement   iii

Introduction   v

Chapter 1: God Works Through You   1

Chapter 2: God Works Through a United Self   7

Chapter 3: God Works Through Agreement   23

Chapter 4: God Works Through the Kingdom   37

Chapter 5: God Works Through the Law   53

Chapter 6: God Works in the Now   77

Chapter 7: God Works Through Thanksgiving   83

Chapter 8: God Works Through Truth   89

FOREWORD

THIS BOOK is for those who have never tried to prove God, those who think they have tried, those who have tried and failed, those who still have hope and for those who are daily proving Him.

This book is for YOU.

INTRODUCTION

THIS BOOK is for those who have never tried to prove God, those who think they have tried, those who have tried and failed, those who still have hope and for those who are daily proving Him. This book is for YOU.

The purpose of this book is fivefold:

1. To bring you into a true relationship with the Laws of God.

2. To give you a tried and true remedy for human ills, problems and needs.

3. To make real the things which you know but have not experienced.

4. To give form and substance to your prayers, treatments and desires.

5. To lead you to discover the Real You.

J. Lowrey Fendrich tells the story of a Chinese philosopher who once came to a missionary and offered to pay him to translate a portion of the New Testament for him each day. The missionary agreed, and for the first lesson opened the Bible and read aloud the words, After this manner therefore, pray ye: Our Father –

To his surprise the aged Chinese stopped him and said, "That will be enough for today."

A year later he returned and said he was ready for the second lesson.

"I thought," said the missionary, "that you employed me to read to you every day."

"I did," replied the old man, "but it took me a year to understand this much."

Introduction

The words in this book are only challenges. The real substance of the lessons is contained between the lines. This means that you should mark, learn and inwardly digest them as you read. As Isaiah said, you will have to wait upon the Lord. You will have to condition your mind through meditation and contemplation. The more you study the lessons, the more light and understanding you will receive. "Mary kept all these things and pondered them in her heart [Soul]."

One of my earliest efforts to put the Truth into print was called This Works. It has long been out of print, but requests for copies still reach me. Those who so faithfully remember the pamphlet will recognize that the material it contained is embraced by this volume.

I have written half the book, but you must write the other half – not on paper but in your daily life. It remains for you to embody the thought in your consciousness. May each hour spent in the study of these lessons bring you manifold blessings!

– ROBERT A. RUSSELL

CHAPTER 1
GOD WORKS THROUGH YOU

YOU ARE entering the area of metaphysics – an organized area with followers working together today under such names as Christian Scientists, Mental Scientists, Divine Scientists, New Thoughters, Religious Scientists and followers of Unity.

It must have been a shock to the world at large when the word science was first associated with religion, for the two fields were for so long almost diametrically opposed, despite the fact that long ago the law and order apparent in the world of nature (growth patterns, the planetary systems, man's physiological structure, for example) were advanced as proof of the existence of a Creator, a Planner, an Organizer. But recent discoveries are compelling scientists in general to conclude that the God of the Christian and the Principle of Law and Order in the natural world may well be one and the same.

Hear what only a few of them are saying now, and read as widely as you will the vast amount of material available on the subject.

Max Planck, the discoverer of the quantum theorem says, "Our impulse to gain knowledge demands a unified view of the world and therefore requires that the two powers should be identified with one another which are everywhere effective and yet still mysterious, namely, the world order of science and the God of religion."

Richard Blair stated, "Lord Rutherford showed more than any other worker that the ultimate structure of matter is energy. Now all energy must become concentrated before it can be translated into terms of power or of matter. It goes without saying that energy cannot transform itself into the immaterial components of the atom. Energy is simply the raw material of creation, lying ready for use by the Mind of the Shaping Spirit; and it is the spiritual formation alone

1

knowledge, wisdom, power, understanding, faithfulness, truth, mercy, goodness, and love.

Metaphysicians also interpret these concepts by such terms as Divine Energy, Principle, Law.

You have taken the first step in your study. Mentally at least you know who and what God is, but of course, you do not know Him until you proveHim for yourself.

The second step in the study of a science is the discovery of its laws – the way it works. Since these are stated definitely in the Scriptures, they are not hard to find. Here we have listed those which are discussed in detail in this book and have also indicated the chapters devoted specifically to each Law.

1. I AND THE FATHER ARE ONE.

    Chapter 2. God Works Through a United Self.

    Chapter 3. God Works Through Agreement.

2. THE KINGDOM OF GOD IS WITHIN YOU.

    Chapter 4. God Works Through the Kingdom.

3. THE LAW OF THE LORD IS PERFECT.

    Chapter 5. God Works Through the Law.

4. NOW IS THE ACCEPTED TIME; NOW IS THE DAY OF SALVATION.

    Chapter 6. God Works in the Now.

5. WITH THANKSGIVING LET YOUR REQUESTS BE MADE KNOWN UNTO GOD. IN EVERYTHING, GIVE THANKS.

    Chapter 7. God Works Through Thanksgiving.

6. YE SHALL KNOW THE TRUTH, AND THE TRUTH SHALL MAKE YOU FREE.

    Chapter 8. God Works Through Truth.

CHAPTER 2
GOD WORKS THROUGH A UNITED SELF

I AND the Father are one.

I know you have read the Story of the Prodigal Son many times but read it again in this search for You.

And he [Jesus] said, "A certain man had two sons. And the younger of them said to his father, 'Father, give me the portion of goods that falleth to me.' And the father divided unto them his living. And not many days after, the younger son gathered all together and took his journey into a far country, and there wasted his substance with riotous living.

"And when he had spent all, there arose a mighty famine in that land; and he began to be in want. And he went and joined himself to a citizen of that country; and he sent him into his fields to feed swine. And he would fain have filled his belly with the husks that the swine did eat; and no man gave unto him.

"And when he came to himself he said, 'How many hired servants of my father's have bread enough and to spare, and I perish with hunger! I will arise and go to my father, and will say unto him, Father, I have sinned against heaven and before thee, and am no more worthy to be called thy son; make me as one of thy hired servants.'

"And he arose and came to his father. But when he was yet a great way off his father saw him and had compassion, and ran and tell on his neck and kissed him.

"And the son said unto him, 'Father, I have sinned against heaven and in thy sight, and am no more worthy to be called thy son.'

desolation came the Voice: "YOU DO NOT NEED TO STAY THE WAY YOU ARE. You do not need to stay in the filth and stench of the pig pen. Leave that old self which has separated you from your birthright. Get back home. Get right with yourself." Do you hear that Voice saying to you, "Let the Creative Purposes of God be expressed in you?"

Then came the transformation. First, the great awakening. "And when he came to himself . . ." Then the great decision: I "will arise and go to my father and will say unto him, Father, I have sinned."

The first step in correcting a mistake is to acknowledge that you have made it. The second step is to seek forgiveness for it – your forgiveness of yourself and the forgiveness of the one you have injured.

The Prodigal is tired of this character he has assumed. Trouble has so hedged him round that he is willing to do anything I "will arise and go to my father, and will say unto him, Father, I have sinned . . . and am no more worthy to be called thy son: make me as one of thy hired servants." This is quite a comedown. He is asking to be demoted. He is willing to do anything. He has lost his false pride. He has recognized the nothingness of personality. He has become receptive to the idea of his place in his father's house, of his true purpose in life.

Notice the difference in his attitude. When he left his father's house, he said, "Give me." When he returned, he said, "Make me." Between these two attitudes is the difference between poverty and plenty. The Prodigal's difficulty, you see, was that he was trying to live "by bread alone." He was like many Truth students who seek answers and results without discipline and without surrender to the Principle, who seek the abundance of the Father's House without developing the Consciousness that produces it.

The Prodigal wanted success, but he got failure. He wanted happiness, but he got sorrow. He wanted thrills, but he got boredom and monotony. He has reached the limit of his endurance. He is reversing all the beliefs, ideals and thoughts that have betrayed him; he is rooting them out. He is determined to be a son again and is ready to do anything to reclaim his rightful inheritance.

Make me. The important thing now is not what he can get from his father, but what the father can accomplish through him. Make me is really the key to the Father's House and no one can enter without it. To be forgiven you must repent. You must reverse your thought. You must change it out of the old condition and keep it changed into the new. It is not enough to feel sorry for your sin. You must surrender it. If you want to be forgiven, you must not only accept the forgiveness (which is already given), but you must stop sinning.

Now comes the great moment. As the son turns toward the father, the father turns toward the son. "When he was yet a great way off, his father saw him and had compassion, and ran and fell on his neck, and kissed him."

There was no penalty for his waywardness, no penance for his sin, no reproof for his profligacy, no probation. The cancellation of his sin was complete.

"Before they call I will answer and while they are yet speaking I will hear", God says. All you need to do is to change your attitude – to take the step homeward. "Eye hath not seen, nor ear heard, neither hath entered into the heart of man, the things which God hath prepared for them that love him."

The son returned to his father's house and there is great rejoicing. Everything is showered upon him – the ring, the best robe, the fatted calf, new shoes, the luxuries of home.

But there was another son who had faithfully stayed at home. With him, too, you are identified. He gloried in his sense of martyrdom. He was filled with self-pity and envy. He grumbled to his father, "Lo, these many years do I serve thee, neither transgressed f at any time thy commandment: and yet thou never gayest me a kid that I might make merry with my friends."

Because that is the only way you can know about anything. What takes place outside your mind, you know nothing about. The Father's House is to you what you are to It, for It is a mental and spiritual state which you establish for yourself.

Do you see now why You have never been in that flesh and blood body of yours and why there is no way in which You could ever get into it? It is because it is in You. The Spiritual You is above the body and not subject to it. You can think about your body, but your body cannot think about you. You can move your body around, but your body cannot move you or itself around. It is governed by your consciousness and your thought about it.

How, then, does your body get so much power in your experience? How does it attract sickness, disease, pain, misery and disorder? Why does it give you trouble? Because you have traded places with it. You stopped being one and you have become two. When you forgot that THE CREATOR AND THE CREATED ARE ONE, that MATTER IS SPIRIT MADE MANIFEST, the Spiritual and the physical ceased to operate together. Personality took over.

We all learn sooner or later that personality is the Prodigal Son in the far country. It is that self which wastes its substance and fills our hospitals, sanitariums and cemeteries. Every day the newspapers tell us about some one whose "me" has gotten out of hand. They go into great detail about the pitfalls, temptations, and dangers which surround him, the accidents, tragedies and mishaps which befall him and the penalties and punishments which are meted out to him. One day he is strong, and the next day weak. One day he is on the mountain top, and the next day he is in the valley. One day he is reaching for the stars, and the next day he is slipping in the mind.

Untouched by Spirit, he believes more in the power of evil than in the power of Good. He misuses and subverts his power; he is slow to recognize God's Presence in time of trouble. Living on the circumference, he finds the greater forces within him dormant. Seeing everything with a view to his own advantage, he closes the channels through which he receives sustenance. When the mind is

16

divided, personality is always in trouble because it makes wrong choices.

Why did Jesus represent personality as living in a far country? Because of its limited material existence. Shut off from its Source, it must of necessity experience both famine and want. Living in a state of apartness, man not only lives beyond his mental equivalents but overdraws his material and physical resources. He does not have the strength to match his proposed effort. Judging according to appearances, he serves his troubles instead of rising above them. Trading his spiritual liberty for material security, he loses both. Living in a state of self-reference, he makes his own frustrations.

But there is merriment and rejoicing in the father's house now. The Prodigal has returned and has been accepted with joy. It is the joy which Isaiah felt when he said, "The mountains and the hills shall break forth before you into singing, and all the trees of the field shall clap their hands," which Job experienced as he heard the Lord in the whirlwind and said, "Where wast thou . . , when the morning stars sang together and all the sons of God shouted for joy?" It is the euphoria which the Greek named to describe the state in which everything is in balance. It is the joy of the shepherd when he found the lost sheep. It is the joy of the woman when she found her coin. It is the joy of a mother when her son returns from war unharmed. It is the joy of a family when a loved one returns home from the hospital healed.

The father's house is a blaze of light. Happiness fills the air. There is music and dancing and feasting. It is a momentous occasion. A reconciliation has been made. A divided mind has been united. The broken has been made whole. Communication has been restored.

Is there anything in the story of the Prodigal Son that is not your story? Well, that depends upon whether you are reading it in past or present tense.

If you have seen yourself in the role of the Prodigal in every circumstance, the wonder of it all has come flooding over you. You know that you can return to your true Home and find that your problems are already solved and your needs already fulfilled.

Do you feel the blessings that are being showered upon you in this glorious homecoming? In the eyes of God, you (the Spiritual You) are the most important individual in the world. You have accepted Heaven as your own state of mind and have lost your sense of separation from God. You know yourself as His son. You are the temple of the living God. You are the center of your universe. You are every man in one.

You are that point in consciousness at which the invisible becomes visible. You are not merely the personal man patched up by medicines, serums, vaccinations and operations. You are the bright, born-anew, fresh, clean, pure, stainless, incorruptible Body of Christ. You are that Self that goes where it will, that knows no barrier, obstacle, circumstance, limitation or condition. You are the unlimited, untrammeled, unsullied, unconditioned Being of Light. Your eye is single to the Truth, and you are one with all creation. You are governed by Divine Intelligence; you are directed by Divine Guidance.

The Freedom of God is your Freedom. The Mind of God is your Mind. The Life of God is your Life. The Power of God is your Power. The Health of God is your Health. The Joy of God is your Joy. The Strength of God is your Strength. You do not beg God to make you whole; you accept the Wholeness which is already yours.

He whom you touch is instantly transformed. Men will call it demonstration, but you know it as revelation. Your demonstrations are assured because you have accepted your divinity here and now. Knowing yourself as Spirit, you demonstrate the Divine Nature. You: do not choose between Good and evil, for you know only Good. You are free as God is free. You are perfect as God is perfect. Having accepted your Oneness, you have no power to feel separate from God.

Knowing that personality can betray you at any time, you have separated yourself from the personal man. You are not conformed to this world. You have spiritualized your Consciousness to the point at which the world makes no more claim upon it. Having been twice-born – born of the flesh and born of the Spirit, you are above the law of the circumstance world and no longer subject to it. You are able to say with St. John, "And we know that the Son of God is come, and hath given us an understanding, that we may know him that is true, and we are in him that is true, even in his Son Jesus Christ."

Reread the story the next time your thought runs like this: "Look at the mess I am in. What am I going to do? Why aren't my prayers answered? Why don't I get results? Why doesn't the Law work for me? Why am I always in debt? Why am I always sick? Why can't I get along with people? Why does everything turn out wrong? I believe in spiritual therapy, but I just don't seem to get anywhere."

When progress slows down, take stock of your mental condition and determine whether you are working from the outside or from the Inside, from the conditioned or from the Unconditioned, from the limited or from the Unlimited, from the relative or from the Absolute.

This parable is not a story to be read. It is a pattern to be followed. It is a rule of Life. "Such were some of you: but ye are washed, but ye are sanctified [cleaned up, made over]." Follow the rule and you get results. In the experience, Self comes alive. By linking yourself to Greatness, you are lifted into Greatness.

It is wonderful to know that you are such an important and unique individual. It is wonderful to know that you are so much bigger and better than you thought you were and that you are entitled to so much more happiness, success, and joy than you have been getting.

You do not have to take my word for all this. Just put yourself in the way of being found by God. "If thou seek him, he will be found of thee." Your desires will be fulfilled. The father said, Son, "thou

CHAPTER 3
GOD WORKS THROUGH AGREEMENT

I AND the Father are one.

On the night before Jesus' crucifixion, He said to His disciples, "I am the true vine, and my Father is the husbandman . . . I am the vine, ye are the branches . . . Without me ye can do nothing." What does this parable mean? It tells you that nobody in this world stands alone. Everybody and everything is related to something else, and each originates with God, the Creator. You can get away from the Father's House, but you cannot get away from yourself. When you think of your personal self as an independent source of power, you lose that power, not because God has turned His back on you, but because you (a branch) have separated yourself from the Vine.

Do you see the lesson Jesus was setting forth in this parable? It was the lesson of relationship. I and the Father are one. This is the message of the New Testament. Your life, your power, your health, your happiness depend upon your acceptance of God. As the branch is dependent upon its oneness with the vine, and the vine is dependent upon its oneness with the ground, so man is dependent upon his awareness and acceptance of his Oneness with the Father Within.

Did you ever read the small print on the stub of a railroad ticket? It says, "Subject to conditions of contract of this ticket and void [that is, not good] if detached." Now apply that statement to life. Think of the many things to which that provision applies: vacuum cleaners, electric lights, fans, toasters, telephones, dish washers, washing machines, refrigerators, door bells. These gadgets are called appliances. They must be applied to something else before they function. Break the connection, separate them, detach them, and they are useless.

The starter in your car is no good unless it is attached to the battery. The water pipes in your home are useless unless they are attached to the reservoir. Your hand is powerless without your arm. Your physical brain is no good without your mind. You are no good without You. You do not enter into your inheritance without your conscious acceptance of your Oneness with God.

This brings us to the great difficulty in spiritual work – the presence of both the human and the superhuman factors in our nature – the two distinct and divergent selves that operate in us.

St. Paul said, "There is a natural body and there is a spiritual body." The natural body is the manifest or physical side which faces the outer world of sense. The Spiritual Body is the Unmanifest side which faces the inner world of Spirit.

You may think of yourself and speak of yourself as being one self, but remember that actually you are two selves. Within you there are two of you – you and Yourself – a human self and a God Self, a personal self and a Christ Self, a lower self and a Higher Self, a little self and a Big Self, an outer self and an Inner Self, a "me" and an "I," a divided self and a United Self, one self on earth and the other Self in Heaven. By yourself – the physical and mental self – you are only half a self. With your spiritual Self, you are a Whole Self. You can succeed in your spiritual endeavors only when the two phases of your life operate together for Good.

Edward Sanford Martin under the title, My Name is Legion, expressed the problem fittingly:

"Within my earthly temple there's a crowd; There's one of us that's humble, one that's proud, There's one that's broken hearted for his sins, There's one that unrepentant sits and grins, There's one that loves his neighbor as himself, And one that cares for naught but fame and self. From much corroding care I should be free – If I could once determine which is me."

That's my problem and it is yours. This split personality must come to terms with itself. The Higher Self must be given an opportunity to organize and control the lower self. The "I" and the "me" must get together.

Since the contrasting phases of your being complement one another and each is an extension of every other phase, you cannot live successfully in one part of your being at the expense of any other part.

It is a great day in your life when you recognize that your struggle is not with the world but with yourself. The conflict is dissolved when you realize that the adjustment must take place in your mind rather than in your environment and then make that adjustment.

The Spiritual You is not disturbed by the passage of time nor by the variations of experience because It is changeless, timeless and immovable. Living on the Higher Side of your being, You are under Grace. You are not righteous, good, well, strong, or prosperous because of some affirmation or statement of Truth, but because You are in Christ.

On this Side of your Being, You are surrounded by a mighty Force which does not know lack, limitation or disease. You are immersed in a Presence which permeates everything and binds all together in one harmonious whole. You live, move and have your Being in a Mind which knows You by what You know about Yourself. You are One with God. You are One with the Source of all creation.

You are One with the Substance of all form. You are greater than anything that can ever happen to you.

Living on the Spiritual Side of your nature, You discover that You do not create anything. You merely become aware of That-Which-Already-Is.

You stop trying to change your world by force, for You know that it is controlled by your attitude toward it. You know that what You release in Consciousness is expressed on the relative plane.

Keeping your attention on the Truth of Being, You are not concerned with turmoil and trouble. You know "All things work together for good to them that love God."

You know that there is not God and health. There is only God manifest as Health. (The chair you are sitting on is not a chair and wood. You cannot separate the wood from the chair. The wood is manifest as the chair.) All Goodness, Perfection, Beauty, Loveliness, and Truth are God made manifest.

There is nothing without Him; there is everything with Him. You are alive because He is alive, free because He is free, rich because He is rich, whole because He is whole, radiant and victorious because that is His nature.

The lower self, composed of body, personality, and intellect, is the sense consciousness that connects you with the outer world.

It was of the lower self that Isaiah spoke when he said, "But we are all as an unclean thing, and our righteousnesses are as filthy rags; and we all do fade as a leaf; and our iniquities, like the wind, have taken us away;" to which Jesus referred when He said, "For this corruptible [lower self] must put on incorruption, and this mortal must put on immortality."

This does not mean that the lower self is destitute of Spirit but that it is spiritually asleep; its potential is unrealized. Only its intellectual and sense natures are awake. Untouched by the Spirit, its greater powers lie dormant.

Did you ever have a straight talk with yourself? Then do so now. Stand before a mirror, look yourself squarely in the eye and ask yourself these questions, listening closely to the answers that you hear.

Who am I? The answer comes back, "I am John Smith." Who is John Smith? "John Smith is my personality."

What is personality? "It is the sum total of all my thinking, feeling and acting on the relative plane. It is that part of myself which I have built up.

It is as the word, persona, indicates, a mask, a sort of false face. It is a false or wrong relation to life. It is my lower self which is in a constant state of change, and being a thing of imagination, it is capricious, unpredictable and unreliable."

Some teachers refer to the "me," or personality, as that part of man's nature which is at variance or out of tune with God.

Personality is the self of duality, always fluctuating between good and evil, heaven or hell, least or famine, darkness or light, joy or sorrow, prosperity or poverty, health or sickness. It is the self that is always getting in your way, the self that is easily hurt, neglected, down-trodden, taken advantage of, the self that allows anger, fear, worry and resentment to poison its whole system.

Functioning from the plane of the relative, it does not know how to embody the Truth of itself. Having lost its spiritual identification, it is always contradicting and denying its good. It does not realize that its failures, limitations and sufferings are induced by its own self- centeredness, self-will, self-love, self-righteousness and self-justification.

Living chiefly on the surface and gathering information from the outer world, it attracts all the annoyances, limitations, inhibitions and miseries of the race. Knowing both good and evil, it is under the law of chance, contagion, disintegration, decay, heredity and environment.

Dwelling in this self, you disturb the normal functioning of the body. You do not solve your problems, for you recognize them as part of yourself.

In a divided mind, your idea of yourself is that you are strong or weak, fortunate or unfortunate, capable or incapable, brave or cowardly, healthy or sick, prosperous or poor, perfect or imperfect, master or slave. You are either happy or unhappy, peaceful or discordant; you move erratically with the tide or against it. You are never consistent, never stabilized, never at peace. You are torn between self-approval and sell-condemnation.

St. Paul said, "The natural man [personality] receiveth not the things of the Spirit of God [for he is in conflict with himself]." The flesh and the spirit, the old man and the new, Babylon and the New Jerusalem are in a state of warfare.

When you think of these two selves as "the self I seem to be" and "the Self I AM," you understand the statement, "There shall be two in the field; the one shall be taken, and the other left."

Now you see why the lower self must be reversed. St. Paul tells us "By grace are ye saved through faith; and that not of yourselves [not of the personality]; it is the gift of God." Grace, the dictionary tells us, "is the state of reconciliation to God through Jesus Christ."

The soul (the subconscious and neutral self) is the repository of experience, thoughts, feelings, memories, impulses and emotions; it bridges the outer and the inner worlds. It is both conscious and subconscious; it is aware or conscious in two directions. The Bible Metaphysical Dictionary tells us, "It touches both the inner realm of Spirit from which it receives direct inspiration, and the external world from which it receives impressions."

Through the soul, you identify yourself with one side of your nature or the other. You identify yourself with the "I" or the "me." On one side of the soul is the fugitive transitory self-lighting, struggling and dying day by day. On the other side is the spiritual Self which was never born, never gets sick and never dies, the Self that says I AM. You designate yourself as carnal or Spiritual, according to the self or nature in which you live.

The soul determines the condition of the body its degree of health, vitality, resiliency. It is the place in which you accept the Truth or deny It. It is the field in which the Holy Spirit does its work.

Where and when does the change-over from the "me" to the "I" take place? There is no place but here and no time but now. You become a new creature not by dying but by accepting your right position in the Law. You make the change when you turn from where and what you seemed to be to where and what You Are. Instead of accepting the corruptible self of the human mind, you see that you are the immortal Self of Divine Mind.

To achieve this integration is the ultimate in spiritual attainment. It occurs when the words of Jesus, "I and the Father are one," become the Truth for you.

But to stay on the Vine, to remain integrated with your Source, you must place first things first. The first of the Ten Commandments is:

"Thou shall have no other gods before me," and Jesus followed it with "Thou shalt love the Lord thy God with all thy heart, and with all thy soul, and with all thy mind."

Jesus said, "If any man will come after me [identify himself with me], let him deny himself [drop his personality], take up his cross [cross out the lower self], and follow me [put on the new man which is Christ]."

Having discovered the Spiritual Self, you let the personal self die. You refuse to act, live and think through the "me." That is what Jesus meant by denying yourself, taking up your cross and following Him.

By constantly yielding the personal self to the Spiritual Self, you crucify the personal self (cross it out) and the Spiritual Self comes forth in resurrection.

The Master gave us the Law back of this creative process in the words, "If two of you shall agree on earth as touching anything they shall ask, it shall be done for them of my Father which is in heaven." There can be no agreement so long as you accept a sense of

29

separation. Nor can there be Oneness, Wholeness, or Completeness. The Spiritual Man has power only as the identity is maintained.

The word Isaiah used is stayed: "Thou wilt keep him in perfect peace, whose mind is stayed on thee." Let the lower self obtrude itself at any time, and the process is interrupted.

St. Paul said, "I die daily." The faster you die to personality, the more quickly the Real You comes to life. On another occasion he said, "I keep under my body [personality] and bring it into subjection." When you cease to believe in a personal man in difficulty and trouble, the saying, "It is no longer I that live but Christ [the Spiritual Self] liveth in me," is fulfilled.

By holding fast to the knowledge that your Real Self is Spiritual, you come at last into the realization of that Self. But you must remember that you have set out to break the most formidable and fixed habit in your life. In reversing yourself, you are not only displacing the false with the True (changing the very basis of your being), but you are transcending the race mind of the world. You will meet barriers, obstacles, delays, disappointments, recessions and setbacks in the process, but these are not the deciding factors in your success. Personality will get back into the saddle from time to time; but if you keep moving toward your Goal, these intrusions are much like the backward and forward movements of a speeding train. It doesn't really make any difference whether you move to the front of the train or to the back. You are still proceeding to your destination.

Separating the Real Self from personality is very much like purifying a glass of muddy water by the introduction of clear water. By the steady dropping of pure water into the glass, the muddy water is washed out. Just so the personal self is displaced by the constant recognition of the Spiritual Self.

Are you ready to take the step? Are you ready to lay down your sense of the personal self and take up the cross which cancels it? Then you must contemplate and study the Self which is waiting to be revealed by your awareness and acceptance. If the personal self is the Spiritual Self unrealized, you must have a clear picture of the Self you wish to express. You must know that this Self IS. You must accept your Oneness with IT.

What does it mean to become one with anything? It means that you become that thing. To become One with the Spiritual Self is to become that Self in action. Jesus knew that man's struggle for health, peace, happiness and plenty would come to an end only as he rid himself of personality. When followers sought to exalt and worship his personality, He said, "Call me not good," realizing that personality is the root of all man's trouble. Then He gave them the remedy: "Now also the axe is laid unto the root of the trees: therefore every tree which bringeth not forth good fruit is hewn down, and cast into the fire." What was He talking about? He was talking about the tree of life – Consciousness.

To reverse the self, you must work with Consciousness. You must not only withdraw your thought and attention from personality with its doubts, tears, worries and sins, but you must also raise yourself to the Christ Consciousness which makes these destructive states impossible. When a tree is cut down at its root, it stops bearing fruit. When the personal self ceases to function in your life, you may be said to have laid the axe unto the root of the trees.

"Acquaint now thyself with him, and be at peace." Acquaint yourself with Him by trying to imagine just how this new Self will affect your life. How will it affect your business, home, job, profession, your family, friends and associates? How would it affect you if right now you were everything you long to be? How would you think if the Ultimate Thinker were thinking through you? How would you act if you accepted God as the only Source of action in your life? How would you feel if Christ felt through you? How would you look if the Holy Spirit looked through you? How would you face difficulties, circumstances and conditions in your new individuality?

realize It, you have no comprehension of Its effect on you or of the changes It would bring into your life.

The Consciousness of your Unity with God is the starting point of every prayer. "If ye abide in me, and my words abide in you, ye shall ask what ye will and it shall be clone unto you."

God can work through you only when your Consciousness and His Consciousness are One. You know then that you are one with All-Power, for you have discovered that there is no power other than that of Mind.

You demonstrate the Kingdom of God because you recognize It as your own State of Mind. You have learned that the purpose of your prayers is to clear the way for your acceptance of your Oneness with Principle. Your success in demonstrating Truth lies in your ability to put all belief in John Smith (personality) out of consciousness.

"All things are yours," Jesus said. That is, all things are manifested through your acceptance of your Oneness with God.

The struggle is now over. You have been born again. You have embodied a new Self. You have discovered a new way of thinking. You have discovered a scientific way of doing things. You have discovered a Law that externalizes only happiness and good. You have integrated the two selves; they are now in agreement and function spiritually.

Who are You? You are the highest of God's Creations. You have dominion. You are crowned with honor and glory. You are the Power which knows no limitation or condition. Your nets are full of fish right in the place where personality said there were none.

Despite your present circumstances, Something in you, Something that is not your body or your brain, Something universal, eternal and indefinable, Something allied to a larger world, Something that never changes, Something that knows You as Itself tells you these things are true.

It is the Real You speaking.

CHAPTER 4

GOD WORKS THROUGH THE KINGDOM

THE KINGDOM of God is within you.

Jesus said, "The law and the prophets were until John; since that time the kingdom of God is preached, and every man pressed into it." He gave an entirely new concept of the Kingdom. The Old Testament uses the word kingdom only with reference to government.

What is the Kingdom of Heaven – the Kingdom of God? Is it a faraway place in the sky to which you hope your soul will retire after it leaves this plane?

Jesus left no doubt in our minds that it is important to understand the meaning of the words, when He made these statements: "Seek ye first the kingdom of God and his righteousness . . . The kingdom of God is within you . . . Except a man be born again he cannot see the kingdom of God . . . Flesh and blood cannot inherit the kingdom of God . . . The kingdom of God is not meat and drink; but righteousness and peace and joy in the Holy Ghost . . . The kingdom of God is not in word but in power . . . No man having put his hand to the plough, and looking back is fit for the kingdom of God."

He made use of many parables as He preached to the multitudes, after saying to his disciples, "Unto you it is given to know the mystery of the kingdom of God, but unto them that are without, all these things are done in parables." These parables help us to broaden our concept of the Kingdom.

He explained His purpose in these words: "Whereunto shall we liken the kingdom of God? Or with what comparison shall we compare it?" Then at various times he made the following comparisons:

37

"So is the kingdom of God, as if a man should cast seed into the ground." [The Kingdom is the Creative Consciousness].

"It is like a grain of mustard seed . . . It is like leaven . . . [The Word of Truth expands into dominion and power as we accept It]." "It is like treasure hidden in the field . . ."

"It is like a merchant seeking goodly pearls . . ."

"It is like unto a net that was cast into the sea, and gathered of every kind."

The Kingdom is entered only as we exercise our power of choice. "All things are yours," said Jesus, but only through the use of volition, the intent to receive, the discipline of will power can we receive from the Abundance that surrounds us, the Supply that awaits our demand upon It, the Substance that is ours. We must take the initiative.

"It is likened unto a certain king who would take account of his servants."

The Kingdom is the Christ-Consciousness in which our forgiveness is assured, for there is nothing to forgive. "Forgive us our debts as we forgive our debtors."

It is like unto a man that is an householder which went out early in the morning to hire laborers into his vineyard.

In the Kingdom of Heaven there is no time but Now. There are no penances, no retaliations when we become laborers in His vineyard.

"It is like unto a certain king, which made a marriage for his son."

Awareness is the first step toward the Kingdom, but Acceptance and Realization must follow if we are to arrive. Preparedness is essential. The guest without a wedding garment was cast out.

"It shall be likened unto ten virgins, who took their lamps and went forth to meet the bridegroom."

Intent is not enough. Preparedness is not a matter of wishful thinking but of action.

"It is as a man traveling into a far country, who called his own servants, and delivered unto them his goods. And unto one he gave five talents, to another two, and to another one."

When we become conscious of the Spiritual Power that is ours, we must accept at the same moment the obligation to use It. As we use It, It becomes greater in our lives. If we do not go beyond the first step of awareness (possession), we lose that Power. "Faith, if it hath not works, is dead. By works is a man justified."

The Kingdom of Heaven to me is like an irresistible and powerful magnet. The magnet is impersonal and unthinking and responds only to certain elements. The Kingdom of Heaven can draw you into It and keep you therein only when you are ready to embody It through your developed awareness. ("I and the Father are one . . . The Father within, he doeth the works.")

But "It is your Father's good pleasure to give you the kingdom." Indeed, He has given It already. The Kingdom of God contains all things within Itself. It is within you, around you, above you and beneath you, but you cannot take possession of It (personify it) until you become conscious of It or aware that It is and that It is in You. You can live in the Kingdom of God and enjoy its benefits only as you build and maintain a consciousness through which It can act.

Jesus likened the Kingdom of God to a mustard seed. It was planted in you in the beginning and grows up in you just to the extent that you recognize It, realize It and cultivate It. If you do not recognize It, cultivate It and act upon It, It is like the seed that fell upon stony ground. God's Power is revealed; It is not reflected nor transmitted. The Kingdom of God must be expressed. Before It can appear, It must have a body. You are that body. "Now are we the sons of God, and it doth not yet appear what we shall be; but we know that, when he shall appear, we shall be like him, for we shall see him as he is."

When you give God your brain to think with, your eyes to see with, your ears to hear with, your mouth to speak with and your body to act with, you will truly know that the Kingdom of God is within you and that you are in It. You will know Him as He IS. You will see yourself as You ARE. You will know that God and man have no separate being – that they are One. "I am in the Father and the Father in me . . . I and my Father are one . . . As thou, Father, art in me, and I in thee." He will be revealed in you just to the degree that you acknowledge the Spirit of all things, accept your identity with It, and thank God for It. The Spirit of a thing (the positive quality) is always good and to behold It steadfastly is to call It forth or cause It to appear. To perceive the Truth, to grasp It, to hold It and use It in the face of all negative appearances to the contrary is Christian totalitarianism.

The word, totalitarian, means, according to Webster, "Of or pertaining to a highly centralized government under the control of a political group which allows no recognition of or representation to other political parties, as in Fascist Italy or in Germany in the Nazi regime."

The word has undoubtedly a disagreeable connotation. And yet I find myself using the phrase, "Christian totalitarianism," over and over in my thinking. No other word combined with the word Christian seems to me to express so adequately the state of Wholeness, Unity, and Oneness produced by the single eye, the one-pointed vision. Since semantics became a frame of reference for our use of words, we realize that a word is nothing by itself, for we interpret it in the light of our experience and thought. The word itself – totalitarianism – has power to me and I propose to right its past wrongs and to make it a good word by preceding it with one of the best of words, Christian. Will you bear with me as you meet it on these pages?

The Truth does not start with man. It is man's answer or response to God. The first line of the first book of the Bible says, "In the beginning God . . ." The first commandment is – "Thou shall have no other gods before me." Jesus said, "Seek ye first the kingdom of God and his righteousness." Because He is first, we are bidden to put Him first in our thought, first in our acts, first in our affection and first in our will. To acknowledge God, to know nothing but His Presence in every person, place and thing is to call the Highest forth. The promise is that "ye shall receive power, after that the Holy Ghost is come upon you [after the prodigal self has been brought into complete cooperation with the Christ Self]."

"I am the Lord and there is none else [I am All-in-All. I am All-Presence.]" When you speak of Omnipresence, you naturally think of God as being everywhere equally present – in all, through all, over all and under all. "Heaven and earth," sang the Psalmist, "are fall of thee." There is nothing but God. There is nothing but His Presence and His Power.

Where do you look to find God? The answer is anywhere and everywhere. God is wherever you look. God is everything you behold. Omnipresence means that God is present in everything and everybody.

Does that statement stretch your credulity? Does it sound inconsistent and far-fetched? Does it mean that when you look at a man whose body is racked with pain and disease, you are seeing God? It certainly does; if you did not have pain and disease in your own consciousness, you could not see them in another.

"Look unto me . . . for I am God and there is none else." The sick man is not sick because he is sick, the poor man is not poor because he is poor; both fail to behold God as He is. Each thinks of himself as something else – something apart from God. They ignore the words, "Christ in you, the hope of glory . . . every man perfect in Christ."

41

Do sickness and poverty change God? Do they affect Him? Not at all. "God hath made man upright," say the Scriptures, and man is just as upright when dying from some dread disease as when he was born. The only thing that ails him is that he does not "see him [GOD] as He is" – does not know Him as the Father, within "who is of purer eyes than to behold evil [sin, sickness]." He does not realize that since God does not know he is sick, he cannot in reality be sick. The only thing that is sick is his viewpoint. Since he demonstrates his belief on all occasions, he has the appearance of sickness. He does not have the spiritual properties within (the Consciousness) which cause God to appear as He IS. What are these spiritual qualities which would save him? The vision and understanding of God as Himself.

Jesus touched on this same point when He spoke of "the Spirit of truth whom the world [human mind] cannot receive, because it seeth him not, neither knoweth him." Most people think and judge with their senses. But "the things of the Spirit of God . . . are spiritually discerned." You recall that Jesus went on to say to his disciples, "but ye know him; for he dwelleth with you and shall be in you."

When you know Him and see Him as He is, you too cannot "behold evil nor look upon iniquity."

"If thine eye be single [one-pointed]," said the Master, "thy whole body shall be full of light;" again He said, "Let your light so shine before men that they may see your good works and glorify your Father which is in heaven." Until the Light shines, God cannot appear.

What we call demonstration is really nothing more than our ability to hold, as a specific image, the positive condition of the negative condition apparent to our senses until the positive materializes. "Let your light shine" means to keep your vision one-pointed toward God. Your mind is the window through which you must see God. It must be kept clean and bright.

"I will look again toward thy holy temple," said Jonah in the midst of his despair. Look again and keep looking until you can see what is actually there. Can you see God in the devil that is making a hell of your life? Can you see Him in the problem which is driving you to distraction? Can you see Him in blind eyes and deaf ears, in the disease that is destroying your body? Do you see Him as He Is? Do you see the positive quality which every negative quality suggests, or do you judge according to the senses? Do you call the undesirable God, or do you call it something else?

What are you trying to escape from? Is it problems or limitation or low visibility? Jesus did not say to make the light shine but to let it shine.

It doesn't matter what you are seeing at the present time; from now on, see it as God. That is Christian Totalitarianism. "If I make my bed in hell, thou art there." Keep reminding yourself that everything and everybody is God. Know that at the other end of every negative condition is the positive; that is God. The Creative Principle is waiting only for the reversal of your thought to bring the Good into being. As you give your mind to the positive, you overcome the negative. Call everything God.

Focus your attention upon the positive which each negative suggests until you know that it is God. Do this in spite of appearances to the contrary. The promise is that "He will keep him in perfect peace whose mind is stayed on thee [upon the positive]." Think positively. Speak positively. Act positively. "Look again and thine eyes shall behold the king in all his beauty."

"If thine eye be single [if you see only God], thy whole body shall be full of light. But if thine eye be evil [double], how great is the darkness!" The single eye is the eye that sees only the Good, the Positive, in everything and magnifies that Good by admitting no other evidence.

Jesus said, "No man, having put his hand to the plough, and looking back, is fit for the kingdom of God . . . He that is not with

What does it mean to "work out your own salvation?" It means to stop building disease and limitation, to give up all the enervating habits of living and thinking which cause these conditions, and to remove all the barriers to the Perfection and Plenty which God is so ready to pour into your life. It means to transform all your negative states of mind into positive states. St. Paul said, "Overcome evil with good." When you do this, nature will return to normal, and you will enter again into perfect balance with God, man and the world. Until you do, your affirmations and study of Truth will do you little permanent good. Like medicine, they may give you a measure of temporary relief, but Health and Supply will not stay with you until you follow that injunction.

God works through you when you recognize that within you is the Kingdom that you seek. He comes to you when you have the single eye.

The riches of His Kingdom are given to you when you think His thoughts and obey His will.

Emancipation (the freedom promised you) is the reward of surrender and awareness. It comes to you when you know the Truth and know that you know, when you are willing to pay the price, when you are willing to "work out your own salvation."

There is only one mental disease – unawareness or ignorance. There is only physical disease from which all other diseases spring – enervation. Enervation is like riding on the rims; it is using nerve energy in excess of normal production. In time it poisons the blood stream and results in so- called incurable disease.

You, as a wise Truth student, will build from the bottom up. You will remove negative mental hazards and correct abnormal and perverted appetites first. "God hath made man upright; but they have sought out many inventions." When the inventions (mental handicaps) have been removed, the Good will appear automatically. You can stop demonstrating, for there will be nothing to demonstrate over. You will be in the Kingdom of Heaven. Heaven is the natural state of man. It is a state of Wholeness, Completion and Perfection; It has no opposite.

A well-balanced mind is anathema to germs, disease, poverty and limitation of every kind. Disease is perverted health; anything that lowers the mental level or lowers nerve energy becomes disease-producing. At the root of every physical disease is toxemia; and at the root of every case of toxemia are the enervating habits which man himself has built into his own mind and body. What is the remedy? Let Nature provide her own antidotes and exercise her own prerogative of healing. As you remove the handicaps and clear away the mental and physical obstructions to the Good that is constantly moving toward you, Nature heals your body and supplies your need automatically.

"I and the Father are one." Supply and demand are always equal when God's mind and man's mind are perfectly synchronized. Knowing the Truth is keeping the mind positive to God, to the Good. God's work is already done. Your work is to keep your mind positive to the Good which He has already bestowed upon you. You do not have to beg for your Good but only to relate yourself to It.

But since God works through consciousness, He cannot supply your needs until you cease to be positive to them. If your consciousness of need is greater than your Consciousness of God, the need must continue to expand under that consciousness.

If the need is to be supplied, your consciousness must be changed. You must lift your vision above the appearance to the fact and keep it there until the Truth forms a Consciousness of Itself in you. Your positive attitude toward the negative state must be transformed into a positive attitude toward the positive state. The subconscious builds into your experience those things which are like your consciousness.

If you send out impulses of discord, inharmony, discontent, poverty, unhappiness, fear and worry, you meet these conditions in your life. The Kingdom is always to you what you are to It; It can never be anything else.

If you are going to change the frequency, or the subjective trend of your mind, you must keep it moving in one direction. You must become receptive to the Good in every experience. You must replace struggle with acquiescence, and competition with cooperation. You must let God appear in you as He IS instead of trying to fashion a God of your own. You were made spiritually in His Image and Likeness (for He is Spirit) in order that He might express through you. When you have made this adjustment, when the trend of your mind has been reversed, you will discover that the pressure of your need was naught but your Supply moving toward you, seeking a positive and receptive state of mind by which to make its Presence known.

The rule is: "In all thy ways acknowledge him [the Truth], and he shall direct thy paths." When you acknowledge God, you do something with your knowledge. Your peril is that you do so little with what you know. You may prefer to debate, listen to, or talk about spiritual ideas instead of acting upon them. You forget that "By works is a man justified." Then you pay the penalty of the conflict between what you know and what you do.

What you need in order to eliminate frustration and disappointment is to rededicate and re-consecrate yourself – to make your relation to God totalitarian. You need to acknowledge God as bigger than yourself and bigger than anything in your world. You need to ascribe to Him the importance and power which you have ascribed to things. Simply holding an idea will not get you anywhere. You must live it and be it. It you do not live it, the Power will not flow into and through you. God is peace, and if you refuse to live a calm, peaceful, composed and poised life, He cannot make His Presence known to you.

What God is, you must be. God is to you what you are to Yourself. When you stop the cause of disease, disease goes away. When you stop the cause of poverty, poverty goes away. God cures you when you, as Emerson said, take your "bloated nothingness out of the path of the divine circuits." You are sick from wrong thinking, from maladjustments in your emotional life and from wrong living. Operations may remove the effects of your wrong thinking, but they do not remove the cause. You remove the cause by reversing your mental attitude from the negative to the positive.

"Choose ye this day whom ye will serve." Just as your needs were produced by negative mental states, so they may all be supplied by your re- collecting, re-mining to and re-joining the Creative Principle. Remember the great awakening of the Prodigal Son? "I will arise and go unto my father." The great trinity in spiritual demonstration is asking, believing, and receiving. In higher metaphysics, we say recognition, realization, revelation. The inward movement is always from the human mind to the Christ Mind, and the outward movement is from God to Christ to man.

Nothing can exist apart from something else. Nothing is good if detached from the Kingdom of God, not even the promises of God. It is in the Kingdom of God (your conscious awareness of the Presence of God) that your prayers are answered, your diseases are healed, your problems are solved and your fear is converted into faith. It is in the Kingdom of God that the Higher Law controls the lower. The Law of Spirit acting through your conscious Oneness with God makes your thought Creative and causes it to take form in your experience. It reacts to your word exactly as you speak it.

What did Jesus mean when He said, "Seek ye first the kingdom of God, and his righteousness; and all these things (What shall we eat? What shall we drink? Or Wherewithal shall we be clothed?) shall be added unto you?" He meant just what the mathematician means when he says two times two are four, or what the metaphysician means when he says "I and the Father are one." Seek that which is eternal and unchangeable. Seek the awareness that the Kingdom of God is All-There-Is, that you are in It, that It is in you, and that It is operating through you now. Then make your thought, your words, and your actions conform to this knowledge. Easy? No,

49

but when you are able fifty-one percent of the time to live this ideal, you are on firm ground.

The knowledge that you are in the Kingdom of God requires you to act, think and feel on the level of this Consciousness. You can, for you know that your every problem is already solved, your every disease is already healed and your every spiritually legal desire is already fulfilled.

But if you in your cleverness and self-sufficiency try to reverse the process, you are claiming that you are wiser than Jesus. If you think you know a short cut, go ahead and seek first the things of the world. "After all," you may say, "there isn't time for all this mental and spiritual preparation, this renewing of the mind, this putting off the old man and putting on the new." But your problems will become more numerous, your load will grow heavier and your demonstrations occur less and less often. Then the realization that you are merely a branch of the true Vine will come, and you will know that you must accept that relationship. "Without me, ye can do nothing."

There is no futurity in the spiritual sense. There is only Here and Now.

You are just as close to the Kingdom of Heaven at this instant as You ever will be. You are enjoying a part of your immortality even as you read this book.

On the Spiritual Side of your nature. You are in the Kingdom of God at all times and the Kingdom of God is in You. You have already inherited everything that belongs to this Kingdom. You need no longer search for anything outside yourself because you know that what you seek is always wherever You are. GOD IS ALWAYS IN INSTANT MANIFESTATION. You experience the Kingdom to the degree that you become aware of It.

You may not now have all the health, wealth, happiness and prosperity that you desire, but the Law is operating for you nevertheless, and as you develop a larger and larger mental equivalent, your desires will materialize to a larger and larger degree. They will become yours in proportion to your capacity to recognize the Kingdom and to live in It.

CHAPTER 5
GOD WORKS THROUGH THE LAW

THE LAW of the Lord is perfect.

"Till heaven and earth shall pass, one jot or one tittle shall not pass from the law, till all be fulfilled."

"Whatsoever a man soweth that shall he also reap."

"And all things, whatsoever ye ask in prayer, believing, ye shall receive." "Whosoever shall say unto this mountain, Be thou removed, and be thou cast into the sea; and shall not doubt in his heart, but shall believe that those things which he saith shall come to pass; he shall have whatsoever he saith . . .What things soever ye desire, when ye pray, believe that ye receive them and ye shall have them."

"The law of the Spirit of life in Christ Jesus hath made me free from the law of sin and death."

"Thou shalt love the Lord thy God with all thy heart and with all thy soul and with all thy mind . . . and thy neighbor as thyself On these two commandments hang all the law and the prophets."

"Ye ask and receive not because ye ask amiss. If thou canst believe, all things are possible to him that believeth," said Jesus to the father who had brought his dumb child to Him to be healed. "And straightway the father of the child cried out, and said with tears, Lord, I believe; help thou mine unbelief."

There we have the Law. What do we do with It? How do we put It to work?

Prayer is so evidently a medium through which the Law works that perhaps we should examine our concept of prayer.

Do you tend to think of prayer only as a formal phrasing of words addressed to the Deity? Then you must get a new concept, for you have the injunction, "Pray without ceasing." You are also told to "enter into thy closet" when you pray. How can you "pray without ceasing" if you must go apart to pray?

We are told to pray to "Our Father which is in heaven" and then told that the Kingdom of Heaven is within us.

Belief is given as an essential in unmistakable terms. But the father of the dumb child frankly admitted his unbelief, and his child was healed.

Jesus gave us a new factor in the words, "Father, I thank thee that thou hast heard me and I knew that thou hearest me always," which He spoke before He bade Lazarus to come forth from the tomb – the quality of gratitude for a request already granted. He had no doubt that a living Lazarus would obey his command although he had been dead four days.

We have a record too of His prayer at Gethsemane and this adds to our concept of what prayer is, for He said, "Father, if thou be willing, remove this cup from me: nevertheless not my will, but thine be done."

His submission to the Will of God is plain, for you remember that He refused to call for the "twelve legions of angels" to save the corporeal body. It is significant too that during this time of tremendous agony He rebuked Peter who "smote off the ear of the servant of the high priest . . . and touched his ear, and healed him." Then too we must recall His words as He hung on the cross, "Father, forgive them, for they know not what they do."

We have then discovered certain essentials to prayer:

1. Intent, a specific desire (one that harms no one but works for the general good).

2. Belief (or a whole-hearted desire to believe), faith, love of God and fellow man, lack of resentment in any form.

3. Knowledge that our desire is already granted and gratitude that this is so.

4. Emotion – The "father cried out . . . with tears . . . Being in an agony, he prayed more earnestly; and his sweat was as it were great drops of blood falling to the ground."

5. "Willingness to surrender to Divine Will." Poets happily define prayer for us:

"Prayer is the soul's sincere desire Uttered or unexpressed, – The motion of a hidden fire That trembles in the breast."

– JAMES MONTGOMERY

"He prayeth best who loveth best All things both great and small. For the dear God who loveth us, He made and loveth all."

– SAMUEL TAYLOR COLERIDGE

"From every place below the skies The grateful song, the fervent prayer The incense of the heart – may rise To heaven and find acceptance there."

– JOHN PIERPONT

We have then two kinds of prayer: the first is involuntary, for it is our habitual attitude toward God – a believing, loving, grateful attitude if we pray aright; the other is the period in which we go apart to clarify our desire, to renew our faith and to express our gratitude.

Since our habitual attitude is expressed in words and acts, this statement of Isaiah is pertinent: "So shall my word be that goeth forth out of my mouth; it shall not return unto me void, but it shall accomplish that which I please, and it shall prosper in the thing whereto I sent it."

"Help thou mine unbelief" might very well be the plea of each of us. We may accept mentally and express verbally our complete identification with the All-Good, but most of us in honesty must admit, as the father did, that we have reservations. Are you free or are you too hedged in by such habitual thoughts as these?

"John has such a cold. I must not get close to him." (Why do you assign power to germs? God is the only Power.)

"I must be careful here or I'll turn my ankle." (Do you want to turn it? Thoughts are things.)

"He's so late tonight. Could there have been an accident? He drives so fast." (Why the negative thought? Something wonderful may have happened.)

"I never could eat so-and-so. It gives me such-and-such." ("Let the dead bury the dead." You live in the eternal Now.)

"I'll not pay this bill right now. I may be short later." (Do you anticipate shortage? Your supply is established in God.)

"He never looks directly at you when he talks. Wonder what is the matter with him. I never wholly trust such a person."

"She talks all the time. Does she have the jitters or is she covering up something?" (Who gave you the right to judge or condemn? You are seeing only personality and not the Real Person.)

"American inventions and ingenuity are certainly falling behind, and it may mean war." (Why fear the evidence of ingenuity which is an attribute of Universal Intelligence belonging to no one person or no single nation?)

Being aware that there are areas in which you must be on guard is a step in eradicating your acceptance of negative conditions. Then, just as the father gave overt evidence of his faith by bringing his child to Jesus to be healed, you too must nullify each fearful thought by an overt action which proves your faith.

The Law of Mind is the Law by which Spirit acts. It is the medium through which thoughts become things or through which invisible ideas become visible effects. Like all other Spiritual Laws, It is universal, neutral and impersonal. The Law of Mind does not choose, decide or select. It knows only how to act. You say, "Be this . . ." or "Do that . . ." and It is compelled by Its nature to obey your word. It knows nothing about what you specify in your prayer any more than the law of gravity knows that the Empire State Building is heavier than a sheet of paper but holds both in place.

Reasoning deductively, the subjective mind (through which Universal Mind acts) does whatever you tell it to do, just as the law of electricity acts when you call upon electric power to be a light, to run a pump, to toast your bread or to wash your clothes. But the Law of Mind will do for you only what it can do through you. The good you seek is not complete until you accept it. When you say, "I can do this," and follow it with the thought, "No, I can't really," you cancel the constructive thought and Accomplish nothing. You cannot compel or force the Law. But you can provide beliefs and concepts on which It may operate. Some one has aptly said, "You do not hold the Law in place; you hold your ideas in place."

Jesus said, "Stand still and see the salvation of the Lord [Law]." Jehosophat said, "Ye shall not need to fight in this battle: set yourselves, stand ye still, and see the salvation of the Lord with you." St. Paul said, "Wherefore take unto you the whole armour of God, that ye may be able to withstand in the evil day: and having done all to stand."

You do not need to struggle or storm the battlements of Heaven to receive your good. All you have to do is to recognize that there is a Law that acts upon your word and speak that word with conviction. Your part is to have a perfect realization of the fulfillment of your desire, to believe that the Law is working, to accept the wish fulfilled, to generate faith in your claim, to let go and let it materialize.

Faith sets the Law in motion. Faith causes the formless to take form. Faith enables you to "stand still" while the Law is doing Its work. "Faith is the substance of things hoped for, the evidence of things not seen." Faith is both the substance and the evidence of every demonstration.

Now make sure that you understand this procedure: Your objective experience is always determined by the subconscious state of your thought. You can consciously impress upon the subconscious mind, the medium through which the Law works, such conditions and desires as you wish to see fulfilled, but you must be specific and definite. Merely wishing for health or supply or any other good thing is not enough. The subconscious mind can bring into your experience, can objectify, only those concepts and ideas which you specifically induce in Mind.

But there is another element in the Creative Process which must not be overlooked. Wonderful as the conscious mind is with its powers of choice, reason and deduction, it is but a fraction of your knowing equipment. Deep down in the subjective world of the Soul are the emotions, or feeling faculties. These feeling faculties are really the steam under the boiler. They generate the power. They form the great driving force of action. They are more powerful than the intellect. You cannot have good results from your prayers or treatments without feeling; your emotions must be involved.

Is this only the dictum of some metaphysician or preacher? No. It comes straight from the Scriptures. Solomon said, "Keep thy heart [feeling center] with all diligence; for out of it are the issues of life." Again he said, "For as he [a man] thinketh in his heart, so is he." Jesus said, "Out of the abundance of the heart the mouth speaketh. A good man out of the treasure of his heart bringeth forth good things."

What is the heart? Were they talking about the physical organ that pumps the blood? No. We say and hear others say, "My heart leaped with joy," or "His heart broke with grief," or "Her heart is heavy." The word heart here refers to the great, unseen spiritual forces of the soul; it is the subconscious mind.

We find this idea in St. Paul's Epistle to the Romans: "With the heart man believeth unto righteousness." And again, "If thou shalt confess with thy mouth the Lord Jesus and shalt believe in thine heart . . ." "Believe in thine heart" – four little words but so full of meaning! Make sure that you understand them. Faith and belief are basically of the heart. The person who prays without feeling is not really praying at all. He is simply mouthing or parroting words.

"That they should seek the Lord, if haply they might feel after him, and find him, though he be not far from every one of us," said St. Paul in speaking of the one blood of all nations of men. Why is the feel important in our search? Because feeling and appearing are two ends of the same thing. When John Wesley said, "I felt my heart strangely warm," great things began to happen for him. Without feeling, there is no warmth, no power, no movement and no birth. Without feeling, the Word cannot become flesh.

When we speak of the metaphysical Law of Cause and Effect ("Whatsoever a man soweth that shall he also reap"), we are really talking about the conscious and the subconscious minds.

The conscious mind is related to the outer world of effect; the subconscious mind is related to the inner world of cause. The conscious mind chooses the idea and impresses it upon the subconscious; the subconscious receives the idea and gives it form. The conscious acts (impresses); the subconscious reacts (expresses). The conscious mind involves; the subconscious mind evolves. The integrating force – that is, the power that connects the concept with the subconscious mind – is feeling. Can you see now why you must never allow yourself to think feelingly of discord, limitation or imperfection, or to become emotionally involved with evil in any form?

Before seed can grow and produce a harvest, it must be planted, watered and cultivated. The planting is a conscious act which invokes the Law. The rest of the process is automatic, mechanical and unconscious. "I have planted, Apollo watered; but God gave the increase." The seed specializes the Law for a definite purpose.

In the realm of Mind, the process is very similar to the law of seed-time and harvest. The seed is a desire. The soil is the subconscious mind through which the Law operates. Acceptance of the desire fulfilled is the planting. The harvest is the desire objectified.

It is not enough to recognize the Law. You must also put It to work. You must apply It rightly and rigidly. The Law says that whatever you impress (that is, accept feelingly as true) upon the subconscious mind will be created for you. It will operate just to the extent that you get yourself out of the way and permit It to work. If It does not work, you have a wrong relationship to It. You are in the way.

It makes no difference whether the impression you have made is good or bad, desirable or undesirable, the subconscious will seek to give it form if your conscious mind feels it to be true. Feeling, whether positive or negative, is always creative and always expressed. What goes in must come out. Feeling is the only way by which ideas can be conveyed to the subconscious mind. This is the Law upon which all demonstration rests.

Do you blame circumstances, conditions and persons for the troubles and misfortunes that come to you? The real culprit is your misdirected feeling. Your world is what your feelings make it. It is made by your habitual moods, emotions and reactions. It can be changed for the better by your entertaining only those feelings which contribute to your highest good.

Emotional disturbances lay the foundation for all kinds of disease. They not only waste energy in anger, fear, resentment, tantrums, regrets, upsets, quarrels and irritation, but they distort judgment, cloud the vision and vitiate the mind. Solomon said, "He that is slow to anger is better than the mighty; and he that ruleth his spirit is greater than he that taketh a city." These words give us a clue as to the magnitude of the task. To master the emotions and bring them under control requires effort, patience, practice, mental discipline, and spiritual understanding.

Much has been written on the subject of controlling the emotions, but in most instances the will is recognized as the key to control. The will, however, rises no higher than the mental and physical capabilities of man.

To get anywhere spiritually, you must have recourse to a Higher Power. You must not only impress upon the subconscious mind the desire to control the emotions, but you must assume the feeling that would be yours if you had already mastered them, knowing that your desire fulfilled already exists in the One Mind.

The reason many conversions in the Orthodox Church do not last is that often only the conscious mind of the individual is converted. The conscious mind accepted the Christ and the spiritual way of life but the conviction was wholly mental. The subconscious was left untouched because the emotions were not involved. The result was a stalemate. The converted conscious mind is cancelled by the unconverted subconscious when the mental acceptance is made without feeling.

St. Paul said, "Be ye transformed by the renewing of your mind." That is, bring them both (conscious and subconscious) under a central control so that they move in one direction toward a focal point, and in the process harmonize all the faculties.

When the subconscious is ignored, the convert is like the man whose starboard turbines are pushing forward while his port engines are backing up. As Kunkel says, "Religion without awareness of the conscious and subconscious . . . is not religion but blind idolatry." Spiritual Therapy treats the mind as a whole, recognizing both the conscious and subconscious aspects. It seeks to produce a perfectly coordinated and integrated person.

What, then, can you do to control your emotions? The first thing to do is to clean up your mind. You can get rid of all the mental clutter of anger, fear, jealousy, envy, hatred and resentment you have accumulated. You can change the patterns of emotional waste by changing your feelings. You can refuse to react negatively to things that annoy and disturb you. You can eradicate your mental

It is true that "if any man is in Christ, he is a new creature; the old things are passed away; behold they are become new."

James Russell Lowell well expressed our obligation to live in the present:

"New occasions teach new duties; Time makes ancient good uncouth; They must upward still, and onward, who would keep abreast of Truth; Lo, before us gleam her camp fires! We ourselves must Pilgrims be, Launch our Mayflower, and steer boldly through the desperate winter sea, Nor attempt the Future's portal with the Past's blood-rusted key."

"If I be a master," said Malachi, "where is my fear?"

The law of the Lord is perfect. Divine Law is the servant of man. It was given to you not only to use in creating those things which you desire but also to enable you to overcome the negative and undesirable conditions in your life. Because God's Law is fixed, rigid, and unchanging, you can always depend upon It. If you use It positively, It will bring only good into your life. If you use It negatively, It will bring evil. The Law is to you what you are to It. It always responds to you according to your believing thought. "As thou hast believed, so be it done unto you. Whatsoever ye shall ask in prayer, believing, ye shall receive." Whatsoever you believe in without doubt is the Law to that thing.

The Law, being impersonal, does not know good or evil. It is so designed that it must produce in you and in your circumstances the image of your beliefs. If you believe that a draught of fresh air has the power to give you a cold, any draught of air is a Law unto that thing. If you believe that golden rod has the power to give you hay fever, for you golden rod is a Law unto hay fever. You will be subject to colds whenever you feel a draught and to hay fever every time golden rod appears because you are subject to whatever you believe in.

If you believe in sickness and health, you are subject to both and will manifest both. If you believe in success and failure, you will be subject to both. There will be times when you will succeed, and other times when you will fail. If you believe in wealth and poverty, you will be subject to both. Sometimes you will have one, and sometimes you will have the other. If you believe that some men are honest and others are dishonest, you will attract both kinds of people into your life. Some will take from you and others will give to you. If you fear thieves, you will attract them to your house. They follow by the Law of your belief. Job said, "The thing which I greatly feared is come upon me, and that which I was afraid of is come unto me." He believed evil would come and it did. What you believe in, you demonstrate on all occasions. By the Law of belief, you have attracted to yourself all that you have now, and by the same Law you have separated yourself from those things which you do not have. The Law has no choice but to obey its own terms.

"I find then a law, that, when I would do good, evil is present with me." Here is the conflict as St. Paul stated it.

At this point, you may be tempted to proceed on the basis of will power. But will is not the method by which you achieve the concept of Oneness. You conceive it with your mind. You are yourself a thought of Creative Mind and share Its power. You use your will, your volition, your intent only to keep your thought fixed on your Realization and to shut the door on anything that attempts to enter and deny that Unity.

Personality asks, "Why do my efforts not work? Why are the results so disappointing? Why is my dream so elusive? Why do I attract so much trouble? Why do things go wrong?" Listen to the answer of Truth. Because there is a Law. "Why are some of my prayers answered and others not?" Because there is a Law. "Why are the important demonstrations so hard to make?" Because there is a Law. "What is it that makes prayer click and where can I find a sure-fire technique?" In Law.

Spiritual Law is like any other law. It works the way you use It. The Law not only does things for you, but It also does things to you, depending upon the way you use It, upon the relationship you establish to It. It will attract or repel, heal or hurt, prosper or penalize, construct or destroy, but It is always limited by your belief. Underscore that statement, for the Law of Itself knows nothing about great or small, big or little, possible or impossible, curable or incurable.

The Law knows only how to act, and It acts only upon your belief. It is to you what you are to It. If you believe in trouble, It will produce trouble. If you believe in delay, It will cause the materialization of your desires to be delayed. If you believe that some demonstrations are harder to make than others, they will be harder.

Like attracts like. "What man is there of you, whom if his son ask bread, will he give him a stone?" asked Jesus. If you plant corn, it will not become squash. The Law of Faith is a law of integrity. You can depend upon It.

Perhaps you did not know that your combined thought and emotion make a demand upon the Universal Substance and that, for the most part, the negative things in your experience are due almost entirely to your unconscious asking. By your failure to collaborate intelligently with God, you may have brought sickness and failure into your life. Have you allowed persons, places and things to determine your state of consciousness and to control your life? Then change the negative conditions by changing your consciousness.

St. Paul said, "Reckon ye yourselves to be dead unto sin [the negative] and alive unto God [the Good]." Instead of living in a negative state of mind, create a positive state and live in it.

"Ask and it shall be given you . . . If thou canst believe, all things are possible to him that believeth." "Intelligent asking and intelligent believing," says Lucius Humphrey, "unite the human mind, the Christ Mind and the God Mind in you, thereby creating whatsoever ye will." Sir James Jeans said, "An idea in the mind produces things outside the mind, and things outside the mind produce ideas in the mind." In other words, you must know what you want. What you ask for must be formed in your mind before it is manifest as experience. You must not only know what you want but, according to Jesus, you must pray from the standpoint of already having what you ask for. You must pray for what you believe you have, knowing that there is no spiritual lack. If what you ask were not already spiritually created and awaiting your demand upon it, you could not receive it.

If you supplicate God, it is proof that you are conscious of some lack in your life. The lack represents a negative condition which can be overcome only a corresponding positive condition. Your asking, therefore, should be in the form of an opposite image held steadfastly in the mind; you thus turn the energy which has been holding you in bondage into new, constructive and productive channels. The new image, if maintained and held steadfastly without opposition or interruption, will counteract all that the negative condition created and produce a new effect.

"Let this mind be in you which was also in Christ Jesus: who, being in the form of God, thought it not robbery to be equal with God. Let every soul be subject unto higher powers . . . For there is no power but of God: the powers that be are ordained of God."

Since your human mind, unaided by a higher power, is insufficient to create or demonstrate anything for itself, it must have recourse to the Higher Intelligence of the God Mind, which is able to do all things. The asking is done, or the image is projected by the human mind. It is then received and held in the soul by the Christ Mind through your faith and belief; from there, it automatically attracts the elements like the elements in itself and is given back to you in form. The purpose of your asking is to unite your human mind with the Christ Mind.

Spiritual demonstration is vastly more than intellectual persuasion; it is knowing – "knowing" that your word does not "return unto you void." It is knowing that all Life, all Power, and all Law are right where you are. "As he [a man] thinketh in his heart, so is he." As you think, so is your experience. Thinking is the determining factor in every circumstance and condition in your life. If you think right, you get good results. If you think wrong, you get bad results.

The verb, think, according to the dictionary, means "To form in the mind; to conceive, imagine . . . to determine by reflection; to think one's way through a difficulty; to get rid of by thinking."

Please remember that definition, for it tells you that your world is made by your thinking. It also tells you that your world can be changed by your thinking. By careful training and discipline, you can educate your thought to accept the statement – GOD, GOOD, IS THE ONLY PRESENCE AND POWER IN MY LIFE.

The metaphysician tells you that your world is no greater than yourself, that it is what your consciousness makes it, that whatever you conceive, believe, desire and feel is realized in your experience.

Your world is only as big, beautiful, wonderful and satisfying as your belief about it. All the Power of God is at your command and you can use It to make your world what it ought to be.

You cannot form too high an opinion of your own possibilities, for you will always receive on the basis of your idea or ideal. God can respond to you only on the level of your mental equivalent.

If this sounds fantastic, let me quote some authorities on the subject. In Man the Unknown Dr. Alexis Carrel says, "The mind is hidden within the living matter . . . It is the most colossal power in the world . . . It is certain that thought may be transmitted from one individual to another." These statements not only stress the importance of carefully selecting, controlling and directing our thoughts, but of protecting ourselves against the beliefs, thoughts and opinions of others.

Hegel, the famous German philosopher, referred to matter as "materialized thought." If this be true, then thoughts are things. By sustained thinking, you can not only produce conditions but also tangible things. Conversely, what you have made by thought can be unmade by redirecting your thought.

In the writings of Marcus Aurelius, we find the statement, "The happiness of your life depends upon the quality of your thought." In the Upanishads we read, "What a man thinks, that he becomes." Shakespeare said, "There is nothing either good or bad, but thinking makes it so." The greatest Book of all says, "As he [a man] thinketh in his heart, so is he." Why in his heart? To remind us that it is not our occasional or passing thought that determines our good or ill, but our habitual, sustained and deep thought.

Judge Troward says, "The stream always has the quality of its source. Thought which is in line with the Unity of the Great Whole, will produce correspondingly harmonious results, and Thought which is disruptive of the great Principle of Unity, will produce correspondingly disruptive results – hence all the trouble and confusion in the world. Our thought is perfectly free, and we can use it either constructively or destructively as we choose; but the immutable Law of Sequence will not permit us to plant a thought of one kind, and make it bear fruit of another."

Your every need is already met. Your supply is established in God. Your only task is to keep the Law, to accept the Supply and to use It wisely. If you have been moving in the wrong direction for a long time, you can now turn around and go in the right direction. It may take a little while for you to get turned around, but turn you must. When Jesus said "Turn the other cheek, Give your cloak with your coat," and "Go the second mile," He meant that you were to go all the way with the Law.

How do you do that? By consciously taking control of your mind and replacing every negative state with a positive state. You have that power; God gave man free will – the power of choice. You must form new habits of thought. When you begin to watch your thinking and your words, you will be amazed at how much of your energy is given over to negatives. Each negative thought must be reversed instantly and consistently until you have a new habit pattern. You must know God as the Creator of your Being and accept your inheritance of "the kingdom prepared for you from the foundation of the world."

Your business in spiritual work is to transmute all the deformities and imperfections which appear into terms of perfection by your positive attitude toward Truth. You do this in the same way that the moving picture operator changes the picture on the screen. He does not deal directly with the picture itself nor with the light; he changes the film. When the film is changed, the picture changes automatically.

Your film is your belief. The screen is your world and your life. It is your body, your home, your friends, your associates, your business and your environment. Your projector is your subconscious mind; it is responsible for what appears on the screen, for your outer circumstances, for what you have and what you are.

Let us suppose that the pictures on your screen are not to your liking. What must you do? Can you change the picture by working with it, by struggling with conditions – stewing, fretting, worrying and fearing? No, for that only creates more ugliness and imperfection in your world. There is only one thing you can do and that is to go within your projector and change the film or image of your thought. You must select in the form of a mental image the picture you want; then you must hold it before you until it expresses itself in the material conditions of your life.

Do you understand that the picture is never on the screen but in your subconscious mind? That it can be changed only by inserting a different film, or belief? There is a Light which shines through your projector; It is always clear and pure whether the picture you project be good or bad. That Light is "the true Light which lighteth every man that cometh into the world." The Light is God-Consciousness. The film, by and of itself, does not and cannot change the Light. It will project any picture you hold before It. When you substitute positive films (positive states of mind) for negative ones, you will get different pictures and different appearances. What the world commonly calls a healing will take place.

Jesus said, "Let your light so shine before men, that they may see your good works," and again "I am the light of the world." Right in the midst of your most trying hour, your deepest sorrow, your most grievous illness, your greatest anxiety and your most terrifying fear, the Light of God is shining, searching out all the dark places in your life. He is in the midst of your greatest failure offering you Success. He is in the midst of your most vexing problem offering you a Solution. He is in the midst of your depleted bank account offering you Supply.

That is paradoxical you say, for how can a God who is love and who perceives only good in His creation allow limitations, deformities and defects to appear? He allows them only in the sense that He has given you free will, that is, volition, and you have chosen unwisely. He has given you the power to see what you wish to see and believe what you wish to believe. If, therefore, you put His pure Light through negative, human films, you will bring out their imperfections.

Is it God's fault when you get imperfect pictures? Do your pictures change God or His Creation? Not at all. "I am the Lord, I change not." How then are your human needs to be met? By transforming your negative states of mind into positive ones. It makes no difference what you may think to the contrary, there is one thing certain and patent to all those who have eyes to see and that is this – a negative state of mind cannot produce positive and successful ideas. If you want desirable results, you must transform every negative state into the positive by knowing that the reversal is the Truth, the negative the false.

You must be so fully conscious of God's Presence and so positive to the good that you are unconscious of anything in your life that is unlike God. Instead of human limitations and imperfections, you must see the divine possibilities in everything and everybody. Instead of sickness, you must see God's Wholeness and you must rely absolutely upon His Power to bring It forth. Instead of situations that seem to demand criticism, you must see God's love and Divine Completion in action.

In His Consciousness, the other fellow becomes your other self. Instead of ignorance, you see Divine Wisdom, Knowledge and Power. Instead of scarcity and poverty, you see God's Infinite and Eternal Wealth. Instead of frustration, futility and failure, you contemplate God's boundless and unlimited Resources. Instead of fear, you practice confidence. Instead of dwelling on weakness, vacillation and indecision, you contemplate God's steadfastness, security and strength.

You must be so secure in your own center of Peace that you can look upon a condition that seems adverse and know that Right Action is prevailing at that very instant. You must be able to look upon apparent limitation and find Plenty, upon discord and find Harmony, upon seeming failure and sense Success, upon physical frailty and see Spiritual Strength.

Have you the bad habit of condemning yourself? Do you belittle your own actions? Self-condemnation is one of the most malignant of negative thoughts. It arises from the guilt sense instilled in us often by early family training, by generations which deemed man "born to trouble as the sparks fly upward," which never let him forget that he was made of the dust of the earth and which threatened the agonies of fire and brimstone at his death.

But when you accept the words of Jesus, you know yourself to be One with the Creator. You are increasingly aware of the Perfection Within and increasingly able to manifest it in your speech and actions. You see that the only purpose of your existence is to express Him on this plane, to be a channel for His action, an instrument for His use.

You rejoice that God knows you as Himself. You know that you do not have to sit in judgment upon others, and consequently destructive criticism has no place in your thought. You recognize

God in every man. Human nature tends to say with the Pharisee, "God, I thank thee that I am not as other men are," but Jesus himself taught the lesson in the first two words of the prayer He gave the world: Our Father. Our not my.

"When Jesus therefore saw his mother, and the disciple standing by whom he loved, he saith unto his mother, Woman, behold thy son! And from that hour that disciple took her unto his own home." Phillips Brooks said, "The power of Christ is thoroughly personal. He fills the single soul with its own inspiration, its own hopes, its own consciousness of responsibility and opportunity. This traditional third word from the Cross is that utterly personal word. The Spirit within brings persons together in mutual love and responsibility. Apart from the intensely touching drama of these two verses from the Bible, there lies the concept that in all our human living we should learn to be mutually helpful if we are to live our religion creatively. Religion's job is not only to integrate a person within himself, but also to integrate him with others in a creative communion."

Jesus said, "On these two commandments hang all the law and the prophets. Thou shalt love the Lord thy God with all thy heart, with all thy soul and with all thy mind . . . and thy neighbor as thyself."

"Love is the fulfilling of the law," said St. Paul. Charity is a synonym for Christian love. When you translate the Law of Love into action in your life you will pray without ceasing. Read I COR. 13. Then read the translation as given by James Moffatt:

I may speak with the tongues of men and of angels, but if I have no love, I am a noisy gong or a clanging cymbal:

I may prophesy, fathom all mysteries and secret lore,

I may have such absolute faith that I can move hills from their place, but if I have no love, I count for nothing;

I may distribute all I possess in charity, but if I have no love, I make nothing of it.

"Love is very patient, very kind. Love knows no jealousy; love makes no parade, gives itself no airs, is never rude, never selfish, never irritated, never resentful; love is never glad when others go wrong, love is gladdened by goodness, always slow to expose, always eager to believe the best, always hopeful, always patient. Love never disappears. As for prophesying, it will be superseded; as for 'tongues', they will cease; as for knowledge, it will be superseded. For we only know bit by bit, and when the perfect comes, the imperfect will be superseded . . . When I was a child, I talked like a child, I thought like a child, I argued like a child; now that I am a man, I am done with childish ways. At present we only see the baffling reflections in a mirror, but then it will be face to face; at present I am learning bit by bit, but then I shall understand, as all along I have myself been understood. Thus 'faith and hope and love last on, these three,' but the greatest of all is love. Make love your aim, and then set your heart on spiritual gifts."

"At that day ye shall knout that I am in my Father, and ye in me, and I in you." "That day" comes at different times to different persons. There have always been individuals whose vision was far ahead of the time in which they lived. They were voices "crying in the wilderness."

You may be one of those fortunate ones who grasp in a flash the idea of the Omnipotent God and their relationship to Him. If you are, you do not need more study. You need only to translate your knowledge into action.

But the human mind seems to learn largely by repetition, as all teachers know. The stony ground that rejected the seed may by the forces of nature become receptive to the next seed that comes its way. So we too often develop Awareness, experience Recognition, and come to the point of Realization by long and persistent study. "Be ye therefore ready also; for the Son of man cometh at an hour when ye think not."

Now when you ask, "Who am I?" do you hear an answer that fills you with confidence?

CHAPTER 6
GOD WORKS IN THE NOW

"NOW" IS the accepted time.

"Say not ye, There are yet four months and then cometh the harvest? Behold, I say unto you, Lift up your eyes, and look on the fields; for they are white already to harvest."

The chief difference between rational theology and false theology is essentially a difference in tense. One claims good now; the other prepares for it in the future. The first accepts what is already here; the second tries to create it. It is the difference between unloading the ship that is already moored at the dock and waiting for a ship to come in. It is the difference between seeking things and having things seek you. It is the difference between seeing things as they are and seeing them as they appear.

Now is the accepted time. It is what you do in the present that counts: the past is gone, and the future is not ready to be acted upon. Give your time, your talent and your power to that which is at hand. Don't waste time upon what you expect to do; turn all your energies upon that which you can do now. Instead of giving anxious thought to the bridge you may have to cross, give scientific thought to the increase of your present ability and power. "Grow in grace and in the knowledge of our Lord and Savior Jesus Christ."

Spiritual strength increases with exercise.

When you are told not to talk about the "four months" which the human mind says are necessary to produce a harvest, you are warned not to put a time limit upon what God can do for you. It means literally that you are not to consider the processes of sowing and growing but to expect the harvest NOW. The grain you wish to gather is already ripe. Do you hear? The grain is ripe. "Lift up your eyes and look on the fields; for they are white already to harvest."

Are you merely a grower and not a harvester? "Having eyes, see ye not? Do you say, there are yet four months and then cometh the harvest?" You must instead consider the difference between Now and then, between Reaping and growing, between Revelation and demonstration, between Being and becoming. What does it mean to "Lift up your eyes and look?" Can you see the Higher Good around you? Can you accept It? Do you petition God to do something for you, or do you thank Him because it is already done? Yes, it is the tense in spiritual work that makes all the difference in the results.

The field is planted, or you must plant it. The grain is ripe, or you must ripen it. Which will you have? There is an old slogan, "Eventually, why not now?" "Beloved, now are we the sons of God. Behold, now is the accepted time; behold, now is the day of salvation . . . The kingdom of God is at hand." It is here now. Your ship is in; you can unload it whenever you choose. The Law of Jesus Christ is a Law of Fulfillment. "I have come that they might have life, and that they might have it more abundantly . . . Ask and ye shall receive, that your joy may be full." Full – do you hear? "All that I have is thine." All is yours NOW and awaits only a corresponding state of your consciousness to be brought into visibility.

"I am the resurrection and the life." You do not have to die to be immortal. You are immortal now. You are living a life that has no end. Right now your life is filled to the brim with luxury, health, wealth, power, happiness, peace, substance, prosperity and contentment. If you are not enjoying your share of these good things, you are thinking through your negative images and causing the Law to bring to you something else. The baptism of the Holy Spirit occurs when you stop being that which you thought you were and begin to be that which YOU ARE. "He taketh away the first, that he may establish the second." To lose sight of the outward manifestation insures the inward Revelation, the fulfillment of the words: "The Spirit of truth . . . dwelleth with you, and shall be in you."

"The kingdom of God cometh not with observation . . . for, behold the kingdom of God is within you." It is within you NOW. It is YOU. "For in him we live, and move, and have our being . . . The kingdom is at hand." It is HERE NOW – the eternal Now and the ever-present Here. That which is already here does not have to come. You cannot go where you are; you can only discover where you are. THAT WHICH IS does not have to be demonstrated but proved. It does not have to be reflected but objectified individually. THAT WHICH IS must be recognized, accepted and used.

IT is not brought to you as a result of your thinking, praying or demonstrating; IT is within you and around you NOW, Your part is to wake up to IT, to become aware of IT.

For "now we see through a glass, darkly; but then, face to face: Now I know in part; but then I shall know even as I also am known."

"Let this mind be in you which was also in Christ Jesus." The human mind, unaided by the Christ Mind, does not see things as they are but as they appear, and appearances are deceiving. "The things of the Spirit of God . . . are spiritually discerned." They must be seen through the spiritual senses. When Jesus said, "My kingdom is not of this world," He meant that you could not express His Life, Health, Substance and Power without His Mind. Since God is Spirit and His Kingdom is a Spiritual Kingdom, you become aware of both through your Spirit.

"Awake thou that sleepest, and arise from the dead [darkness], and Christ shall give thee light." Since the darkness of human understanding is the only problem there is, you can overcome it only as you let in the Light. As the Light grows, you will see things as they are. You will see them "face to face." You will know as you are known. "Ye are the light of the world [your world]. A city that is set on a hill cannot be hid."

"Having eyes, see ye not? And having ears, hear ye not?" asked Jesus. To try to discern spiritual things without His Mind (Light) is like searching in the dark to find an object. Without the light, you cannot see at all or you may see but the dim outlines of the objects in the room; but you cannot discern clearly anything that is there. The objects are all there, but you do not see them as they are. Without the light, you have a limited vision of everything in the room.

"Then the eyes of the blind shall be opened, and the ears of the deaf shall be unstopped." The vision of the single eye is true. In the midst of the most imperfect, malformed and pain-racked body is Perfection. Within the meanest, most murderous man alive is God. Under the most crippled enterprise is God. Inside the most helpless situation is God. He is both the visible imperfection and the invisible Perfection. There could be no imperfection without Perfection. The imperfections are but your failure to see clearly the Eternal Perfection which never changes. Reality does not come into full view until you let the Light operate. "Wherever you can vision perfection," says Celia C. Cole, "you can attain it." As far and high as you are able to see, so far and high can you go. Your ability is always equal to your vision. The trick, of course, is to be able to brush aside appearances, to go right through them to the Spiritual Fact back of them. To realize what the Spiritual Fact is (as a scientist knows what his formula is) and to stand upon it immovable, undisturbed (no matter what appears) is your part. By using the power you have to see Good, you increase your power to see God. By observing the working of the Law in every happening, you develop spiritual perception.

When you go to Honolulu, you do not have to demonstrate the climate, plants, swimming and volcanoes. You have only to open your eyes to what is already there and enjoy it. When you are in Hawaii, you are under the laws of Hawaii and no longer under the laws of your home state. What would you think if you saw a man in Honolulu walking around its streets affirming that there was a Honolulu and that he was in it, affirming the sunshine, orchids, gardenias? Wouldn't you think that there was something wrong with such a man? Wouldn't you think it strange that he did not accept and enjoy what he already had?

Then what about the Truth student who spends his days and nights declaring the Truth and affirming that he is in the Kingdom of God but continues to live his former life? How can one enjoy Honolulu unless he accepts the life it offers? And how can you enjoy the Kingdom of God unless you accept your life in It? You do not need to take a plane or a ship to arrive at the Kingdom of God. You do not even need to get anyone to help you reach It. You are already there. But you must be more aware of it than you are of the external world.

When you jump into a pool of water, it is the business of the water to make you wet. The water substantiates itself. When you go to the North Pole, it is the business of the climate there to make you cold. When you go to the tropics, it is the business of the tropical climate to make you warm. The climate substantiates itself. When you accept your place in the Kingdom of God (keep your mind focused on the Good – the Positive), it is the business of the Kingdom of God to supply you with everything you desire and need. "All I have is thine." The term used is "is," not "shall be." When you know that you are in the Kingdom of God, you have the freedom promised you. "Ye shall know the truth, and the truth shall make you free."

In the Kingdom of God, you do not declare that there is no sickness or poverty, for there is nothing for negatives to act with or upon. The Perfection of the Kingdom of God is all that exists. "It is your Father's good pleasure to give you the kingdom." It is yours as long as you remain in It, as long as you are positive to the Good, just as it is the business of water to keep you wet as long as you stay in the water. However, just as you lose sight of the things in Honolulu when you return home, you lose sight of the things in the Kingdom of God when you go back to the human mind.

Jesus said, "Continue ye in my love . . . Abide in me." The secret is to keep the eye single, to allow no division in the mind, no deviation from the path. He will keep you in a perfect state of health, wealth, peace, power and abundance if your mind is stayed upon Him – upon the Good – upon the Positive.

"When the elements of time and space are eliminated, all our ideas of things must necessarily be as subsisting in a universal here and an everlasting now," says Judge Troward. Metaphysical principles embody this thought in these words: GOD IS EVERYWHERE EQUALLY PRESENT. GOD IS IN INSTANT MANIFESTATION.

Is there anything unusual about a potter producing pottery, a jeweler producing jewelry, a baker producing bread, a composer producing music? Is there anything unusual about a man with the Mind of Christ doing the works of Jesus?

Is there anything strange about instantaneous healing or an immediate answer to prayer? Or the answer preceding the prayer? Before they call I will answer, and while they are yet speaking I will hear."

Time is a man-made measure. Even in our lifetime we have seen its values change. The telephone, the telegraph, improved means of transportation, radio and radar enter into our concept. Around the World in Eighty Days was once so startling a thought that most persons living at that time deemed it impossible; today science announces an object that travels around the globe in speed that is beyond our comprehension. "Beloved, now are we the sons of God."

CHAPTER 7
GOD WORKS THROUGH THANKSGIVING

WITH THANKSGIVING let your requests be made known unto God. In every thing give thanks.

There is an infallible method of practice which will not only produce new ideas and increase your power but which will also give you the means by which all personal problems can be solved and by which all personal desires and wishes can be fulfilled. It is such a simple formula that a child can use it successfully. It is the Law of Asking, Believing and Receiving all in one word – Thanksgiving. "Faith is the substance of things hoped for; thanksgiving is the evidence of things not seen." Faith and thanksgiving go hand in hand; they are the handmaidens of the Lord.

We have seen the necessity of bringing the two selves into complete cooperation. No other method is so successful in accomplishing this as the simple practice of thanksgiving. If rightly practiced, it effectively harmonizes the lower self and the Higher Self.

"Enter into the gates with thanksgiving, and into his courts with praise; and be thankful unto him." The key to successful practice and living is to be found in gratitude and praise; conversely, the greatest thieves to happiness and abundance are ingratitude and complaint. After all the metaphysical theories have been written and all the philosophical platitudes spoken, the thing that really sets the Law in operation is thanksgiving. When everything else fails, thanksgiving succeeds. It succeeds because it is mathematically correct. It is the method which Jesus used.

If there is such a thing as a shortcut to Heaven, you will find it in the practice of thanksgiving. Genuine gratitude opens your entire being to God and frees your mind from the undesirable negative thought which has made it impossible for you to accept the things for which you have prayed.

When Jesus said, "Pray without ceasing," He was not telling us to beg, supplicate or beseech God continually to do certain things for us but to cultivate a deep sense of whole-souled gratitude. To be perpetually thankful for everything is to fulfill the command, "Pray without ceasing."

The prayer of faith, or acting upon what we already have, is the most effective of all methods of prayer. It is really praying in three ways at the same time, or more literally speaking, it is three prayers in one. It is the prayer of Asking. Believing and Receiving; it is Recognition, Realization and Revelation.

Jesus proved that He understood this method of prayer when, before there was any tangible evidence of the answer, He said, "Father, I thank thee that thou hast heard me. And I knew that thou hearest me always." It was not His words alone that caused the Power to come into manifestation but His Faith that what He thanked the Father for was already there. "Father, I thank thee" is the full recognition and realization that the action you wish is taking place at the moment of your asking. It doesn't make any difference what systems you use, how much you know or how much you pray, the object of your prayer cannot become yours until you have thanked God for it.

There are many definitions of prayer but the most comprehensive one is that it is the Practice of the Presence of God. This, of course, is the prayer of thanksgiving.

First, you mentally lay hold of the Good you desire. You recognize that It is here now. Then you practice absolute confidence in God's desire and ability to bestow It and in Christ's activity to bring It forth by expressing your gratitude.

"The prayer of faith, shall save the sick," said St. James. "Be of good comfort, thy faith hath made thee whole," said Jesus. What is faith? It is a settled state of feeling. It is absolute confidence in God, in your word and in the Law. When your faith in God is absolute, your prayers work for you because you are a channel for Divine Action. Instead of your seeking things, things seek you. When you have become a magnet for Good by establishing a positive state of mind within yourself, nothing can keep your Good from finding you. You now attract It by virtue of what you are. Having entered into a state of balance or unity with God, you attract from the outer world everything needful for a perfect harmonious existence. "He that hath the Spirit [positive state of mind] hath the sign also." God's riches flow to you from every source, and whole-souled gratitude opens wide your mind to receive.

Is there a momentous and important decision which you must make? Do you need guidance and wisdom? Then say to the need each time it comes to your mind, "Father, I thank Thee." See how quickly guidance will come.

Is there a problem in your home, office, business or personal life which you have been unable to solve? Then say each time you think of it, "Father, I thank Thee." See how quickly the solution appears.

Are you depressed, anxious or tearful over a situation which you do not seem able to control? Then repeat the words, "God, I thank Thee." See how quickly your confidence will be restored.

Are you so sick that nothing seems to do you any good? Then say every time your sickness comes to mind, "Father, I thank Thee." See how soon your health will improve.

Are you in debt and need money? Say, "Father I thank Thee" each time the need comes into your mind. See how quickly supply materializes.

Give thanks instead of complaining. Give thanks instead of fearing. Give thanks instead of worrying. Give thanks instead of wondering. God is very present help in time of trouble, but He cannot help you unless you accept His help on Spiritual terms. Help comes through your positive state of mind and through your attitude of praise and thanksgiving.

The moment the emotion of gratitude touches you, your spirit lightens, your burden grows less, your smile comes more readily. Let gratitude become a basic part of your consciousness and the joy to be found in the Kingdom will be revealed to the world through you.

"That they [believers] might have my joy fulfilled in themselves, said Jesus. Note the words: my joy. Thou halt made known to me the ways of life; thou shall make me full of joy with thy countenance. . . The kingdom of God . . . is righteousness and peace and joy in the Holy Ghost."

Look up the reference in any concordance to such words as joy, joyful, joyfully, glad, gladness, merry, and happy.

Surely among the signs that "shall follow them that believe" are the joyful countenance and the merry heart.

THINGS TO BE REMEMBERED ABOUT THANKSGIVING

1. The ultimate goal of all spiritual practice is to be so fully conscious of God's Presence that you are unconscious of anything unlike God.

2. Since God is the Source of all supply and the giver of every good and perfect gift, the closer you live to God the more spiritual benefits you will share.

3. The best method for living close to God is the practice of whole-souled gratitude. The mind that is always grateful never knows need.

4. If you are grateful for the good things you have now, you keep your mind open to receive Good. When you are truly grateful for everything, you constantly receive more of everything.

5. A consistent attitude of thanksgiving brings the mind of man and the Mind of God into perfect reciprocal action.

6. The grateful mind is a power-full mind. It always accomplishes everything it sets out to do. It is tireless, buoyant, joyous, alive.

7. The thankful mind is always positive to the good. It looks for the best and so brings the best out of everything. Seeing only the good, it causes everything to produce good.

8. The grateful soul is cumulative. The practice of thanksgiving keeps the mind in the ascending tendency, and the higher the mind goes, the greater is its possessions. The more grateful it is, the more power it has.

9. The thankful soul lives in the NOW and expects everything in the present. It does not live in the future.

10. In love is love reflected. The grateful person sees the best in everything, expects the best of everyone, finds something good in every situation, and consequently draws friends, opportunities and supply toward him.

11. The grateful soul is always a satisfied soul. Drawing its Substance and Life from within, it is always complete.

12. The thankful soul is a productive soul. Living close to the Source, it not only attracts more but produces more in every sphere of activity.

13. The grateful soul is a regenerative soul. In the consciousness of real gratitude, a healing force is always at work counteracting negative conditions.

14. The grateful soul is a balanced soul. In whole-souled gratitude, supply and demand are always equal.

15. The grateful soul is joyous.

CHAPTER 8
GOD WORKS THROUGH TRUTH

YE SHALL know the truth, and the truth shall make you free.

In mathematics, we say two times two equals four. That is a fact on the mathematical plane. In metaphysics, we say "Ye shall know the truth and the truth shall make you free." That is a fact on the Spiritual Plane.

"I am having such a terrible time with my nerves. How can I meet this condition?"

"How can I develop a prosperity consciousness?" "How can I stop worrying?" "How can I stop smoking?" "How can I stop drinking?" "How can I rid myself of fear?"

"How can I overcome my tendency to colds and my susceptibility to changes in the weather?" "How can I meet friction and misunderstanding in my home?" "How can I heal my insomnia?"

Is your current problem here or have you some pet problems of your own that make you unhappy, that keep you disturbed and insecure?

It doesn't make any difference what the particular problem or difficulty may be, the treatment is to take your thought away from the condition or problem and place it upon the Spiritual Reality of the solution.

There are many forms and methods of prayer and treatment but the essential in all prayer is to know, and know that you know, that what you have asked in prayer is already yours. You have no doubt repeated those words many times, but the mere repetition of words does not change or accomplish anything. That is why you are warned against "vain repetitions" and "much speaking." If you are not free before you say you are free, the parroting of the words will not make you free.

Many students think, as the heathen do, that "they shall be heard for their much speaking." They storm the battlements of Heaven with affirmations, decrees and declarations only to find that words by themselves do not establish the Truth.

Jesus did not say, "Ye shall affirm the Truth," or "Ye shall talk about the Truth." He said, "Ye shall know the truth [have a Consciousness of Truth]." When He said, "All things are yours," He was stating a fact. If you do not have the consciousness of Truth, if It does not become a fact in your life, you cannot take possession of the things that are yours.

Now meditate on this statement for a few moments: "Ye shall know the truth, and the truth shall make you free." Does Jesus say that you are going to become free without any effort on your part? No, there is a condition which must be fulfilled before you receive the promised freedom. You must provide the outlet. "Know the truth," and God will act through you to make you free. The Truth which is already established and in action will make you free when you know that Truth. It will make you free through your awareness and your realization that you are already free.

Since you desire this freedom, you will pray for it. Voluntarily or involuntarily, you pray for what you most want.

But prayer is not for the purpose of fulfilling your desires or satisfying your needs; it is to provide within you a consciousness through which they can be met.

"Effective prayer is the voluntary concentration of our own psychic energy toward fulfilling the benefits already potential in us," says Jeremy Ingalls in The Galilean Way.

Prayer conditions the mind, quickens the consciousness, and lets God through; it clarifies the vision, strengthens faith, removes obstacles and lets in the Truth. The Good is already in manifestation, but you must mentally see It, recognize It, and develop an attitude of acceptance, an intention to receive It, before It can become a part of your experience.

You become free by realizing that God is at the Center of your being, by letting "this mind be in you which was also in Christ Jesus." And what Mind is that? It is the One Mind common to all men—the Mind in which we "live, and move, and have our being." Get this concept firmly fixed in your consciousness and you have grasped one of the basic teachings of Jesus. The Mind that you use and the Mind that I use and the Mind that everybody uses is the One Mind.

It is true that you may use this Mind for both good or evil; It is Power which you direct. It has no limitations, no troubles, no difficulties; It is never disturbed. And what does that mean to you? It means that your Mind has no limitations, troubles or difficulties and that It is never disturbed. It is your human mind that is disturbed, the mind which Jesus said must be denied. When you align yourself with Mind, when you accept that Mind as God operating in You, when you know Yourself as a thought of that Mind, the human mind ceases to limit and frustrate you and you are free.

Who are you? Why is it important to know who you are?

Listen to Ernest Holmes: "In and by the one Mind you are known as a point of Consciousness; therefore, you have the power to know whatever you choose to know. Your knowing is done, with and in this One Mind, since there is no other mind. Consequently, you and this Mind are One and the same thing." This is WHAT YOU ARE. When you grasp this concept of the Real You, you have taken a long step toward true freedom.

The God-Mind in you is perfect, but the human mind in its misdirected thinking causes the very Mind of Perfection to produce imperfection, the Mind of Freedom to produce bondage, the Mind of Health to produce sickness, the Mind of Plenty to produce poverty, the Mind of happiness to produce misery. That is why Jesus said,

"Ye shall know the truth" and why St. Paul said, "Now we see through a glass darkly."

Before the full-orbed glory of your Real (Christ) Self can appear, before God can work through you AS YOU, your human mind must be stilled. You must consistently know the One Mind. Knowledge is always integral with the knower; as you train your human mind to accept One Mind, One Presence and One Power, it loses its function as a separate mind.

Jesus said, "Whosoever shall not receive the Kingdom of God as a little child, he shall not enter therein" and also "Ye must be born again." The child has no preconceived opinions; he does not argue or reason about Truth. He readily accepts and believes in that which he has never seen. To become "as a little child" demands that you set aside all your belief in two powers and identify yourself with the One Mind.

Do you know the Truth, or are you still living in the pigsty of the human mind? What is Truth? We speak glibly of the Truth. We call ourselves Truth students, but who among us can define It? We are like the bewildered Pilate who many years ago asked Jesus the same question.

There are many definitions of Truth but one of the most comprehensive is that given by Richard Lynch: "Truth is the ultimate, illimitable, infinite power pervading all existence. It is the hidden harmony of life; the single thread of meaning that runs through and connects all things; the unchangeable principle that controls the universe."

"To this end was I born," said Jesus, "and for this cause came I into the world, that I should bear witness unto the truth." Truth is "That-Which- Is." The human mind deals with the "was-ness" or "maybe-ness" of life. Truth deals with the "Is-ness" of Life. Since It includes within Itself all that is past, present and future, there is nothing opposed to It, nothing to divide It, nothing to deny It, nothing unlike It, nothing different from It. Since It is Universal, there was nothing before It and there can be nothing after It.

It is ever-present, indivisible, unchangeable, permanent, stable and reliable. Having nothing unlike Itself by which to divide Itself and containing all within Itself, It is Unity; It is Oneness.

The Truth that makes you free does not free you by the passage of a Higher Potential into a lower potential, but by your realization that there is only one Potential. There is merely "IS-NESS" and that which It claims Itself to be.

The major theme of Jesus' teaching was the dominion of man – For "thou hast made him a little lower than the angels, and hast crowned him with glory and honour. Thou madest him to have dominion over the works of thy hands [the whole creation]." This settles forever the idea that you are the creator of anything. You can by virtue of your dominion call forth That-Which-Already-Is, but you cannot add to or take from It. It is already Whole, Perfect and Complete.

The dominion which God gave you is not physical but spiritual. Your real dominion lies not in the mastery of your difficulties, ills and limitations but in your power to bring into visibility the Good which already Is. On the relative plane, you seem to create, change, heal, invent or demonstrate things, but what you really do is to become aware of a Law that has always existed and live by It.

You have to recognize that your power and accomplishment depend upon the Source and that you are merely the channel through which It moves. This is being "poor in spirit;" true humility is the willingness to say, "I can of mine own self do nothing . . . But the Father that dwelleth in me, he doeth the works."

In Truth, your healing is already accomplished, your prayer is already answered, your problem is already solved, your cup is already full, your desire is already fulfilled, your need is already met. If you are not enjoying the blessings which are so freely and lavishly given, it is because you do not know that they are already in manifestation. You demonstrate them by becoming aware of them; this, in Jesus' words, is knowing the Truth.

You do not rid yourself of unwanted things by trying to force them out of your life, but by knowing the Truth of Being. You do not demonstrate Health by manipulating matter, adjusting matter, by pouring matter into matter or by operating on matter. You simply become aware of Health as a Reality here and now.

If Health were not already yours, all the doctors, surgeons, and metaphysicians in the world could not give It to you. By meditating on the perfection of the Real Self – the Self that was never born, never gets sick and never dies, you become aware of That "which was, and is, and is to come," and you are healed.

What has happened in this so-called process of healing? Nothing but a change in your belief regarding Health. You have reversed the order of your thought from what you seemed to be to what You Are and the undesirable condition has ceased to exist for you.

Turning from appearance to Reality, from falsehood to Truth, you have found that You have dominion.

The Truth that makes you free is your realization that You are One with God ("I and the Father are one") and your recognition that your thought is creative. "As he [a man – that is, you] thinketh in his heart so is he." When you accept the fact that your thought is creative, that the mind which you use is God-Mind, you can, by directing your thought, cause the harmony you desire to be objectified in your affairs, your body, and your world.

Why is it necessary for you to gain a consciousness of Truth? Because it is the only way you can be freed from human bondage and limitations. False thinking binds you, but Truth liberates you. It relieves you of allresponsibility by bringing God into the Center of your Being. Your only responsibility, therefore, is to know the Truth – not only when you are in difficulty or have some problem that you cannot, solve but "without ceasing."

Truth is a way of knowing, living, thinking and acting. If you want God to walk with you, you must be willing to walk with God. You cannot be a Son of God and a son of the world at the same time.

The watchword of every Truth student should be "For this cause came I into the world that I should bear witness unto the truth." When you can rise above the human mind with all its misdirected thinking and become the Truth in Action, you will see as God sees and know as God knows. See what? See the perfect Creation which God pronounced good. Know what? Know that It has never been and never will be anything less than perfect.

How do you become a witness to Truth? By consistent and unceasing effort to live and think according to Principle. The needs and problems listed at the beginning of this chapter reflect a limited and imperfect adjustment to life. When you become the Truth in Action, problems cease to exist for you.

There is a vast difference, you see, between knowing the Truth and talking about It. A declaration of Truth is merely what you affirm. The Truth is what God imparts to you – the awareness of His Presence. The distinction is clear. Words without the awareness of God back of them have no power. They are just so many empty shells. It is the feeling of the Presence within your own being that gives them life. "The Father that dwelleth in me [my awareness of the Presence], he doeth the works."

God does not come any closer to you because you repeat a hundred times, "He is here." You experience His nearness by feeling the warmth of His Presence. He becomes active in you when you discover that you are One with Him. You can repeat many times a day, "God is my help in every need," and receive no help at all; but you cannot say "God is my help in every need" with the conscious awareness of His Presence without receiving immediate help.

Do not interpret the words of Jesus, "Take no thought for your life," to mean that you are to do nothing, that you are to live a thoughtless state of existence; nothing could be further from the

Truth. If to "take no thought" means to do nothing, how are you going to become conscious of your Oneness with God? How are you going to become aware of His Presence? How are you going to "pray without ceasing?" How are you going to know the Truth that makes you free? The only possible way to achieve anything is by taking thought.

"Take no thought for your life, what ye shall eat, what ye shall drink, what ye shall wear withal" refers to your concentration with material needs. "Seek ye first the kingdom of God and his righteousness and all these things shall be added unto you," promised Jesus. Put first things first.

Affirmations are reminders that what you seek is already here. They deepen your realization (the affirmative factor in demonstration) of that which is already true.

"Who by taking thought," asked Jesus, "can add one cubit unto his stature?" Who by taking thought can add anything to his life? You tell me. Tell me about that sickness you are trying to heal. Why is it perpetuated from one day to another? What is it that sustains your sickness? What is it that holds it to you? The power of your thought. Take your thought from your sickness, and it ceases to exist for you. How do you know that this is true? Because the more you think of your sickness, the worse it becomes. When your body is well, it is out of your thought.

Walter C. Lanyon says, "A state of perfect health is a state of unconsciousness as far as the body is concerned. The moment the misdirected thought lays hold of a portion of the body, that part of it becomes sick, and is constantly in thought.

"Man has only to turn to the realities of existence; that is, that he is already perfect (not that he is going to be), that he is already prosperous (not that he is going to be, for the time element has nothing to do with God's plan), to see it manifest itself."

"All things are yours," Jesus said. Then you do not "take thought" about a new ice box, a television set, a larger income or a healthy body; you simply realize that your needs are already met. You begin by knowing your Oneness with God, who makes the crooked places straight and the rough places smooth. "He will keep him in perfect peace whose mind is stayed on thee." When you keep your mind stayed upon God, you are praying without ceasing. You are moving with the Power which restores you to the harmony of Divine Mind and to the consequent adjustment of all your affairs.

Knowing the Truth is not only maintaining your awareness of God but also realizing that it is His "good pleasure to give you the kingdom." No longer do you need to struggle and fight to work things out. No longer do you beg God to save or to help you. You become aware of your True Self, and your awareness nullifies any evil circumstance or condition that may be apparent in your life. Not in the frantic and futile efforts of the human mind but "In quietness and confidence shall be your strength."

John Oxenham once said, "Do your part; leave it with God to spread the leaven." What is your part in spiritual work? You have the answer in Jesus' words, "that I should bear witness unto the truth." Your part is to provide God with a clear channel through which to do His work. Your responsibility is to "bear witness unto the truth."

There is a Way in which your prayers can be answered. To follow that Way is to get results; to fail to follow It is to get consequences. There is a Way through which Truth can appear, and there is a way in which It is blocked. You can have the answers to your prayer only as you fulfill the conditions of Its manifestation, that is, by developing a Consciousness of Truth.

It doesn't make any difference whether you are praying, building a house, digging a well, selling merchandise, surveying land, engineering a highway, constructing a bridge, building friendships or conducting a court of law, the necessity of obedience to the Law of Truth holds good. You meet the conditions and you get results.

"Ye shall know the truth, and the truth shall make you free." That is the Law. It is just like saying that white is white, black is black and two times two are four. You, as a true metaphysician, will not reason, argue, petition or beg God for what you already have. You will acknowledge that you have it, thank God for it and take it. To you, GOD-IS-GOD. Knowing that spiritual things are spiritually discerned and working from the basis of Christ Mind, you will not think of false combinations. To you, God IS.

You realize the Law.

Is your body sick? Is your pocketbook empty? If you admit these conditions, you are saying that two and two make five or something else. If you proclaim the He, it doesn't change the fact. If you proclaim the Truth, it doesn't change the fact. What does your declaration change? It changes nothing but yourself. It can do nothing but bring your own mind into alignment with Truth.

Truth is the positive quality of every negative condition. Did two and two make four before or after you said that it did? Did your declaration of the Truth make It so or was It so before you proclaimed It? Jesus said, "Father, I thank thee that though hast heard me" before there was any tangible evidence of the answer to His prayer. He was not trying to create something but was stating a fact that was part of His Consciousness.

How can you know the truth of a negative condition apparent to the senses? By identifying the positive condition which the negative has reversed and staying your mind upon It until It forms in you a Consciousness of Itself.

How does the Truth make you tree? By moving you with the Power and enabling you to direct It into positive channels.

"I am the Lord, I change not." The Christ is "the same yesterday, today and forever." If you say, "I am sick," "I am poor," "I am unhappy," the Law maintains you in sickness, poverty and unhappiness. "Awake, thou that sleepest, . . . and Christ shall give thee light." Knowing the Truth is bringing the conscious and subconscious minds into perfect alignment with Fact. The Fact takes form when you become the Truth in Action.

As you refuse to entertain negative thought, you call forth the higher use of the Law for the fulfillment of your desires. As your mind becomes more and more positive to the Truth, material conditions will improve. To obey the Law and use It positively and constructively is the rule for all successful achievement.

You can see that the best way to get rid of the devil in your life is to supplant it with Good, that the best way to destroy the consciousness of poverty is to cultivate the Consciousness of Plenty, that the best way to destroy the consciousness of sickness is to cultivate the Consciousness of Health. The wise gardener works to make his crop so abundant that it will stifle or crowd out the weeds. If you spent all your time in trying to get rid of the negatives in your life and did nothing more, you would finally succeed in producing a state of consciousness devoid of goodness as well as evil, and it would be good for nothing

St. Paul said, "Overcome evil with good." When you introduce the positive idea and hold to it, the negative goes back to its native nothingness. "Except ye be converted . . . ye shall not enter into the kingdom of heaven." What is conversion? It is merely a change of allegiance from the negative side of life to the positive side. It is both a change of mind and a change of self. It is not acquiring new things but shifting your attitude so that you can use the things which you already have. When you are converted, you align yourself with the Positive and make It supreme.

Jesus knew how devastating negative thoughts can be and how easily they creep into your consciousness and steal away your faith, security and peace of mind. He knew too, that when the heart is troubled, depressed and downcast, the entire man is likely to be troubled, depressed and downcast. He said, "Come unto me all ye who are weary and heavy laden and I will give you rest . . . Let not your heart be troubled."

When you are in the downbeat of discouragement, turn all your thoughts in praise and thanksgiving to God. Place your troubles in His hands and they will diminish until they disappear. Recognize that God never leaves a job half done and that "He which hath begun a good work in you will perform it until the day of Jesus Christ."

Deep down within you is the knowing, believing, accepting, realizing, grateful You who daily and hourly is increasingly able to reveal the Truth of Being.

Many requests come for the right words to use for meditations, particularly in the first moments alter wakening. There is no set pattern; I can give you no model to be copied. Each person must find his own key to the Silence. I offer the statements that follow because they in part summarize the Truth of Being that I hope you have been able to accept in our work together.

I KNOW THAT I AM NOW A NEW PERSON. I HAVE YIELDED THE OUTER SELF TO THE INNER SELF. I HAVE CROSSED OUT THE OLD MAN FROM MY NATURE. I ACCEPT MYSELF AS THE SPIRITUAL MAN IN RESURRECTION. I AM STRONG AND OF GOOD COURAGE. I AM EQUAL TO EVERY NEED. I ACCEPT ONLY THE GOOD AND RECEIVE ONLY THE GOOD, AND I AM GRATEFUL TO THE POWER THAT HAS REVEALED THESE THINGS TO ME.

I REALIZE THAT I AM UPHELD AND SUSTAINED BY THE MIGHTY PRESENCE AND POWER OF GOD, AND THAT GOD-POWER IS RELEASED IN ME, CHANGING EVERYTHING THAT NEEDS TO BE CHANGED, HEALING EVERYTHING THAT NEEDS TO BE HEALED AND ADJUSTING EVERYTHING THAT NEEDS TO BE ADJUSTED.

MY NEEDS ARE FULFILLED THROUGH MY CONSCIOUSNESS OF ONENESS WITH GOD. THE SPIRIT OF THE LORD GOES BEFORE ME MAKING EASY, SUCCESSFUL AND STRAIGHT MY WAY. I HAVE LIMITLESS FAITH IN MY UNCONQUERABLE SPIRIT AND KNOW THAT THERE IS

NOTHING IN ME THAT CAN OBSTRUCT THE DIVINE CIRCUITS OF HEALTH, HAPPINESS AND SUPPLY. I AM VICTORIOUS OVER EVERY PROBLEM. I AM COURAGEOUS IN DANGER AND EQUAL TO EVERY EMERGENCY. MY WORD DISSOLVES EVERY DOUBT AND REVERSES EVERY FEAR. I HAVE COMPLETE CONVICTION THAT MY EVERY DESIRE WILL BE FULFILLED.

I KNOW THAT I AM IN THE KINGDOM OF GOD NOW. THAT WHICH I SEEK IS SEEKING ME. THAT WHICH I HAVE LOST WILL BE FOUND. THAT WHICH BELONGS TO ME WILL COME TO ME. THAT WHICH IS HIDDEN WILL BE REVEALED. MY BODY IS RENEWED, REVITALIZED, STRENGTHENED AND HEALED. I MANIFEST PERFECTION IN VERY ORGAN, IN EVERY NERVE, IN EVERY CELL AND IN EVERY FUNCTION.

I AM IN COMPLETE UNITY WITH All GOOD, FOR I THINK ONLY CONSTRUCTIVE, POSITIVE, HELPFUL AND LIFE-GIVING THOUGHTS. I MOVE WITH THE MIND OF CHRIST. THE DIVINE CIRCULATION FLOWING THROUGH MY MIND IS NEVER DIVERTED, DILUTED, INHIBITED, CONGESTED OR RETARDED. EVERYTHING I THINK, SAY OR DO IS QUICKENED INTO PERFECT RIGHT ACTION. MY THOUGHT STREAM IS PURE AND PERFECT AND AUTOMATICALLY DISSOLVES EVERYTHING UNLIKE ITSELF.

TODAY I HAVE UNSHAKEABLE CONFIDENCE IN THE LAW OF FAITH AND IN MY POWER TO DEMONSTRATE IT. I AM ALIVE WITH THE LIFE OF GOD. I KNOW EXACTLY WHAT TO DO AND HOW TO DO IT. I AM GOVERNED BY LAW IN EVERY THOUGHT AND WORD, AND I ACT WITH ABSOLUTE CERTAINTY AND CONVICTION.

TODAY I AM RADIANT WITH THE LIGHT OF GOD. I AM THAT POINT IN CONSCIOUSNESS THROUGH WHICH GOD SHINES. I AM ABLE TO SEE GOOD WHERE EVIL SEEMS TO

BE. I AM UNLIMITED, UNFETTERED, UNTROUBLED AND UNBOUND. I AM TRIUMPHANT, VICTORIOUS AND FREE.

I AM CENTERED IN THE CALM AND PEACEFUL SPIRIT OF GOD. I AM AT PEACE WITH MYSELF, WITH MY WORLD AND WITH THOSE AROUND ME. I REJOICE THAT THE PEACE OF GOD FLOWS THROUGH MY WHOLE BEING. I ACCEPT THE WORDS OF JESUS AS SPOKEN DIRECTLY TO ME-PEACE I LEAVE WITH YOU, MY PEACE I GIVE UNTO YOU . . . LET NOT YOUR HEART BE TROUBLED, NEITHER LET IT BE AFRAID.

TODAY I ACCEPT ALL THAT I HAVE DESIRED AND PRAYED FOR. THERE IS NOTHING IN ME TO DOUBT OR DENY THAT THE GOOD I AM SEEKING ALREADY EXISTS AND THAT IT WILL MAKE ITS APPEARANCE IN MY EXPERIENCE. NO FALSE EVIDENCE CAN DIM MY FAITH OR PREVENT ITS REALIZATION. I AM UNDER THE GOVERNMENT OF DIVINE LAW. I USE THIS LAW AND IT BECOMES THE LAW OF MY INDIVIDUAL BEING. THE LAW OPERATING THROUGH ME MAKES MY THOUGHT CREATIVE, AND MY EVERY SPIRITUALLY LEGAL DESIRE IS SATISFIED.

TODAY THE CHRIST WITHIN ME MAKES ALL THINGS NEW. I HAVE LET GO OF THE LESSER SELF IN ORDER TO EXPERIENCE THE GREATER SELF. EVERY ADVERSE, LIMITED THOUGHT, BELIEF OR CONDITION IS DISSOLVED IN THE WHITE LIGHT OF TRUTH. BELONGING TO GOD, I NOW BELONG TO MYSELF. HAVING TRADED THE UNREAL FOR THE REAL, HAVING SEPARATED THE FALSE FROM THE 'TRUE, I MOVE FROM A NEW BASIS. GOD ACTS THROUGH ME BECAUSE I HAVE ACCEPTED THE KINGDOM OF GOD AS MY OWN STATE OF MIND. HE ACTS THROUGH ME AS ME.

THIS IS THE DAY THAT THE LORD HATH MADE. I SHALL REJOICE AND BE GLAD IN IT. TODAY I SEND OUT

LOVE TO ALL I MEET BY MY WORDS, BY MY ACTIONS, BY MY APPEARANCE. I EXPRESS MY OWN JOY IN MY ATTITUDE TOWARD EVERY PERSON I MEET. I GO FORWARD TO MEET MY GOOD. I SPEAK NO EVIL AND HEAR NO EVIL IN WHAT IS SAID TO ME OR AROUND ME. I AM CONSCIOUS OF PERFECTION IN ALL I LOOK UPON, AND THAT PERFECTION IS OBJECTIFIED IN MY EXPERIENCE WITH THOSE WHOM I WORK WITH OR THOSE WHOM I CASUALLY MEET. I KNOW THAT, CONSCIOUSLY OR UNCONSCIOUSLY, WE ALL HAVE THE SAME PURPOSE TO EXPRESS HIM ON THIS PLANE – TO BE A CHANNEL FOR GOOD. I DO NOT HAVE TO WAIT FOR THE FUTURE TO SEE MY GOOD MATERIALIZE. I LIVE IN THE ETERNAL NOW AND THE EVER PRESENT HERE. THIS IS THE DAY THAT THE LOUD HATH MADE.

SELF-ANALYSIS

The quiz that follows is designed not to determine how much you know about Truth but how well you live the Truth that you know. Remember that you are trying to find out how you rate as a Truth student and how well you apply the Truth in your everyday life. The score is significant to you, not to anyone else.

1. Are you obedient to the command, "Thou shall have no other gods before me?" Do you look to God for all your Good?

2. Do you accept the fact that everything in your experience, whether good or bad, is the direct result of your own state of mind?

3. Do you understand that there is nothing outside of you which acts upon you or has power over you? Do you understand that there is no evil in the universe which can touch you without your consent?

4. Are you convinced that nothing comes into your life except as the state of your consciousness attracts it?

5. Do you make sure that all your prayers and treatments are accompanied by realization?

6. Do you realize that nothing in your world is safe or secure unless you have the Consciousness of the Presence of God?

7. Do you know God as You, as the Life of You, as the Mind of You, as the Christ of You, as the Truth of You?

8. The Jews are looking for the first coming of Christ. The orthodox Christian Church is looking for the Second Coming, but Jesus says, "Lo, I am with you always, even unto the end of the world." Do you understand that Christ is eternal, and perpetually awaits man's recognition and acceptance?

9. In the days of His flesh, Christ appeared as Jesus. Are you aware that now He appears as you and I?

10. Are you aware that prayers or treatments without the Consciousness of your Oneness with God do not get any further than your own belief? That results from this kind of praying are not from God but are the result of your faith in your human self?

11. Are you aware that when you pray or treat you must raise your consciousness above the physical plane for the prayer to be effective?

12. After you have claimed your Good from the Universal Storehouse, do you stop thinking of your need and let God supply it?

13. Do you have a lively expectation of the fulfillment of your desire? Do you have an intent to receive, an attitude of acceptance?

14. Do you apply the principle that the thing you desire must be given up (surrendered in its entirety) before you can have it?

15. Have you cultivated a healthy and vigorous disinterest in the negative?

16. Do you cleanse your thought of everything that would prevent the Good from getting into your life?

17. Do your intellect, your will and your feeling agree with the word that you speak?

18. When you declare the Truth about a condition or seek to bring some specific good into your life or into the life of another, do you have a clear and definite mental pattern of the end you wish to accomplish without any involvement of the method by which it will come?

19. Do you still outline when you pray, that is, do you try to figure out the ways and means by which the prayer can be answered? Or do you leave the means to the Law?

20. Do you always determine whether your desire is spiritually legal before you pray? Are you sure that it harms no one and that it is in accord with the Divine Will?

21. Do you understand that the Law of Life operates through your mental equivalents or beliefs? Do you put your whole trust in the Law?

22. When you declare the Truth, do you become still to the point at which there is no barrier between yourself and It?

23. When you employ Divine Power are you certain that there is no difference between big and little, between curable and incurable, between possible and impossible?

24. Do you understand that it is your conscious Oneness with God that channels your Good to you? That you have His Mind, His Life, and His Power only as you maintain your contact with Him?

25. Recognizing that will can accomplish nothing worthwhile by itself, do you keep it employed in rejecting any suggestion of the negative?

26. Are you striving to let the lesser self die daily? Are you consistently trying to set aside all the false beliefs of the human mind?

27. Are you so positive in your attitude toward Life that you can say as one having authority, "Thou art made whole . . . Lazarus, come forth . . . Stretch forth thine hand . . . Be thou opened?"

28. When you apply Truth to a problem, do you concentrate upon Truth and not on the problem? Do you stick to It or do you allow appearances to throw you off the track?

29. Do you understand what it means to find your life by losing it? Do you know that what you really lose in the process is not your life but a false sense of being?

30. When obstacles rise up in your path, do you see them as self-created conditions and not as entities? Do you fight and resist them or do you agree with them quickly and reverse them?

31. Do you always expect instant and perfect results from your prayers? Do you have an attitude of joyous expectancy?

32. Do you believe that all healing is instantaneous healing and that there is no such thing as gradual or partial healing? That healing comes when the call reaches Christ?

33. Do you understand that the power of your word is in your conviction that God is thinking and acting through You?

34. When you start to work on a problem, do you think of the Answer and not the problem?

35. Do you use your will only to keep your mind above the level of your problem and on the level of the Answer?

36. Do you accept the fact that if anyone injures or offends you, it is because in your consciousness you have the capacity to be injured or offended?

37. Do you understand that the Eternal Now the only time there is, that heredity, race beliefs, and the past have no power over you?

38. Understanding that denial of evil is a recognition of evil, do you root out troublesome thoughts by instantly reversing them?

39. Do you expect everything you do to prosper? Do you identify yourself with success and refuse to entertain images of defeat, doubt, fear and failure?

40. Do you know that Good is the only power in your life?

41. Do you understand that your prayers and treatments reveal Truth, but do not create It?

42. Do you make sure that there is no coercion, compulsion, force or persuasion in your spiritual work?

43. When you pray, do you draw your desire out to a specific point? That is, when your desire has become a demand upon Universal Substance, is the demand clear and definite?

44. Are you aware that all prayer and treatment take place within and upon your own mind?

45. Do you thank God for the fulfillment of your desire before there is any evidence of it in your experience?

46. Do you have an absolute conviction that that which you seek is seeking you? That that which belongs to you by right of consciousness cannot escape you?

47. Are you confident that the word which you speak "will not return unto you void but shall accomplish that whereunto it is sent?"

48. Do you have absolute faith that your word is powerful enough to penetrate and dispel every inharmonious condition and to dissolve every negative thought?

49. Do you begin your prayers and treatments with a deep realization of the Presence of Christ? Do you sit quietly in the Silence until you are immersed in peace and feel that elevation of Spirit within you that you know is the Christ?

50. Have you given up all idea of trying to correct or change things in your body, affairs or experience knowing that the Consciousness of Truth will appear in the outer world as the thing which you need?

Now tally up your answers. It you answered ten of these questions in the affirmative, you are making progress and should be encouraged to become more accurate and proficient in your application of Truth principles. If you answered twenty-five, you are well on your way. As you persevere in knowing the Truth, your ability to live It will increase.

Now as I write the last words of this book, I must admit that I know a great deal more about you than I stated earlier in this book.

You may be a member of the congregation of Epiphany Church whom I know very well, or one of the many members I do not know personally. You may be an occasional visitor to our service or a stranger from out of town.

You may be tall or short, fat or thin, blonde or brunette, married or unmarried, physically perfect or handicapped. I still know the Real You.

I know You as I know Him and as I know Myself.

You are a Child of God, a Thought of Mind. You are One with your Creator. I see You strong, efficient, beautiful, happy, peaceful, loving, and loved.

Since You know that You partake of the attributes of your Creator – God, who is Life, Light, Love, Intelligence, Wisdom, Understanding, Peace, Power, Beauty, Order and Joy, I know that You are accepting the Consciousness which embraces these attributes.

I know now that you are a persistent seeker, or you would not be reading the last page of this book. And so I know that you are increasingly aware that there is a Place for you in the Sun, that you are increasingly able to use your knowledge of the Way to that Place, that your realization of your Oneness with God is enabling you to live in It more and more habitually.

And as I know the Real You, I pray with perfect confidence that my prayer is already answered that you will continue in His Love.

CPSIA information can be obtained
at www.ICGtesting.com
Printed in the USA
BVHW090958200123
656618BV00006B/705